P9-DBM-193

100
perfect pairings

small plates to enjoy
with wines you love

Jill Silverman Hough

WILEY

JOHN WILEY & SONS, INC.

Printed on acid-free paper ♾

Copyright © 2010 by Jill Silverman Hough. All rights reserved

Photos Copyright © 2010 by Lucy Schaeffer

Published by John Wiley & Sons, Inc., Hoboken, New Jersey

Published simultaneously in Canada

No part of this publication may be reproduced, stored in a retrieval system, or transmitted in any form or by any means, electronic, mechanical, photocopying, recording, scanning, or otherwise, except as permitted under Section 107 or 108 of the 1976 United States Copyright Act, without either the prior written permission of the Publisher, or authorization through payment of the appropriate per-copy fee to the Copyright Clearance Center, Inc., 222 Rosewood Drive, Danvers, MA 01923, (978) 750–8400, fax (978) 750–4470, or on the web at www.copyright.com. Requests to the Publisher for permission should be addressed to the Permissions Department, John Wiley & Sons, Inc., 111 River Street, Hoboken, NJ 07030, (201) 748–6011, fax (201) 748–6008, or online at http://www.wiley.com/go/permissions.

Limit of Liability/Disclaimer of Warranty: While the publisher and author have used their best efforts in preparing this book, they make no representations or warranties with respect to the accuracy or completeness of the contents of this book and specifically disclaim any implied warranties of merchantability or fitness for a particular purpose. No warranty may be created or extended by sales representatives or written sales materials. The advice and strategies contained herein may not be suitable for your situation. You should consult with a professional where appropriate. Neither the publisher nor author shall be liable for any loss of profit or any other commercial damages, including but not limited to special, incidental, consequential, or other damages.

For general information on our other products and services or for technical support, please contact our Customer Care Department within the United States at (800) 762–2974, outside the United States at (317) 572–3993 or fax (317) 572–4002.

Wiley also publishes its books in a variety of electronic formats. Some content that appears in print may not be available in electronic books. For more information about Wiley products, visit our web site at www.wiley.com.

Library of Congress Cataloging-in-Publication Data:

Hough, Jill Silverman.

  100 perfect pairings : small plates to serve with wine you love / Jill Silverman
Hough.

      p. cm.

   Includes index.

   ISBN 978-0-470-44631-7 (cloth)

   1. Appetizers. 2. Cookery. 3. Wine and wine making. I. Title. II. Title: One hundred pairings.

   TX740.H693 2009

   641.8'12--dc22

                                        2009017333

Printed in China

10 9 8 7 6 5 4 3 2 1

dedication

To my husband,
my hero,
my best friend
—I'm so lucky to be paired with someone as perfect as you

acknowledgments

A huge hug of gratitude to my agent, Jennifer Griffin, and everyone at The Miller Agency. It makes all the difference in the world to have someone else in your corner—especially someone as savvy and supportive as Jennifer.

A big thank you to Linda Ingroia, and everyone at John Wiley & Sons, for helping my idea blossom and for having it turn out so beautifully. Thanks, too, to Lucy Schaeffer and her team and to Elizabeth Van Itallie—I'm proud to be the beneficiary of your obvious talents. Thank you to Laura Norcia Vitale for my author photo.

Anne Baker, Mia Malm, and Constellation Wines—thank you for very generously donating wine to my project. Thanks, too, to Peter Marks for helping to make it happen.

Kevin Toomajian, Wine God, thank you for helping me look like I know something. I truly appreciate your friendship, and your expertise.

To my recipe tasters—John Danby, Pam Fischer, Susan and David Norman, Andrea Stupka, and Beck, Tom, Kelse, and Meghan McIver—you've contributed to these pages, and me, immensely. Thank you for being on my team, and for proving that people are willing to participate, excited even, if you just ask them.

To all the editors I've had the good fortune to work for and to all the cooks I've had the good fortune to work alongside—thank you for the education.

Finally, thank you to my grandmothers and my parents for giving me the gift of good food. Thank you to my family—especially my parents, brother, in-laws, and husband—and ALL my fabulous friends for your love and support, in this and all things. Thank you, mostly, for the delicious life I lead. I love you.

contents

about this book

You are holding in your hands possibly the first-ever food and wine pairing book decidedly *not* written for food and wine geeks.

This book is for everyday wine drinkers, regular folks who like a glass of wine with a meal or with friends, or both, and who also like to eat good food and have that food complement the wine, and vice versa.

If that describes you, this book is for you.

In fact, in this book I will purposefully *not* attempt to educate you about the finer points of food and wine pairing. The general points, sure. But one of the things that drives me crazy about most food and wine pairing books is that their authors seem to think you have to *learn* about food and wine pairing before you can *do* food and wine pairing and then *enjoy* delicious food and wine.

But you don't have to know *how* to do food and wine pairing to enjoy it. You don't have to know all the dishes that pair well with, say, Zinfandel, or why they do, to make one of them and appreciate it with a glass of Zinfandel.

So with this book, you get to cut to the chase. Just open the Zinfandel chapter, pick a recipe, make it, and pour yourself a glass of Zinfandel as you sit down to eat.

Another thing that drives me crazy about most food and wine pairing books—they recommend wines that most everyday wine drinkers have never heard of or can't afford. Try this with a Spanish Albariño or that with a Puligny-Montrachet, they'll say. Or they'll mention a familiar wine, but recommend a specific producer or year. What if you can't find Robert Mondavi Winery's 2005 Oakville Cabernet Sauvignon? Guess you can't make that recipe.

So with this book, I've stuck to twelve of the most basic varietals, wines you can find at great wine stores and also at the supermarket, at all price points. I couldn't resist throwing in a few that may be sort of new to you, because they're good food wines, but they're still easily and affordably available wherever you buy your wine.

And every recipe in each chapter will go with every bottle of that varietal. Some recipes might work better with certain *styles* of, for example, Chardonnay, but they'll all work with Chardonnay. If you know that your particular bottle of Chardonnay is buttery or that it's crisp, great. If not, don't worry about it. At all.

All of this isn't to say that there aren't really, *really* perfect food and wine pairings out there, ones that are a magical match between a very specific bottle of wine and a very specific dish. I'll never forget one incredible evening at a San Francisco restaurant, when my husband and I had a killer combination of smoked sea bass and Riesling. I wish I could remember what Riesling it was, so I could reproduce that positively perfect pairing again and again. But I still enjoy smoked sea bass with Riesling, all kinds of Riesling.

The bottom line is, if you'd like to *enjoy* food and wine pairing without having to learn everything there is to *know* about food and wine pairing, this book is for you.

If you know a lot about food and wine pairing and simply want more recipes to enjoy with the wines you drink, this book is for you.

If you don't even know what I mean by a perfect pairing, this book is for you.

YOU DON'T HAVE TO BE RICH TO ENJOY FOOD AND WINE PAIRING
Certainly, one of the attractive things about good food and good wine is that they're associated with "the good life."

But that doesn't mean that you have to spend a lot of money to enjoy them. In fact, one of the great things about wine is that it's made in every style and for every budget.

There's room for everyone at the table.

---

so what exactly *is* a perfect pairing?

Some say a good food and wine pairing is one where neither element overwhelms the other, where they're complementary.

Some say a good food and wine pairing is one where the food doesn't change the taste of the wine, or if it does, it changes it for the better. You take a sip of wine, you take a bite of food, and then you take a sip of wine again—and the second sip doesn't taste any different than the first. Or if it does taste different, it tastes better—the bitterness was softened, say, or the wine got fruitier.

I say that how you recognize a good pairing is that you put food and wine together in your mouth and you either like it or you don't. It's a purely personal decision and, really, not that complicated.

does every pair have to be perfect?

I'm pretty sure you know this, but—there are no food and wine pairing police. So rest assured that every pair absolutely does not have to be perfect.

Sometimes alongside your food, you enjoy whatever wine is on hand, or you try a new wine, or you simply drink what you know you like, perfection be darned. One recent evening, I had a burrito for dinner and wanted a glass of wine with it. There was an open bottle of Chardonnay in the fridge. Is Chardonnay and burritos a perfect pairing? Probably not. Did I enjoy my meal nevertheless? Absolutely.

Perfect pairings shouldn't be some ideal that you have to strive for or that, one day, you might finally achieve.

Rather, think of perfect pairings as an arena to play in. Don't have them be a burden. Have them be something to explore and enjoy.

how to use this book

Even though I won't attempt to teach you everything there is to know about food and wine pairing, it doesn't mean you won't learn a lot. Just by flipping through, say, the Pinot Noir chapter, you'll notice that many of the recipes have earthy ingredients, like mushrooms and olives, and sort of through osmosis you'll learn that those kinds of flavors tend to work with Pinot Noir.

Should you want to learn more about a varietal, look at the information at the beginning of each chapter, which will include the varietal's broad characteristics and tips for pairing recipes with it.

You'll also notice that sprinkled throughout the book are Food & Wine Tips. Again, they'll help you learn about food and wine pairing through osmosis, without having to consciously remember anything. Pay attention to them to the degree that you're interested in knowing more.

the recipes

All these small plates recipes are relatively easy to prepare, and many are super-simple, making them great vehicles for exploring food and wine pairing.

What do I mean by small plates? Well, sometimes a small plate is simply less than a meal. Maybe you enjoy it as a snack, finger food, or appetizer. Or maybe you serve several at a party. Sometimes a small plate can be served as a first course salad, soup, or pasta. And sometimes a small plate is simply a smaller or sharing-sized portion of a main course entrée or side dish, enjoyed on its own or combined with others to make a multidish small plates meal—like you might get at a small plates or tapas restaurant. If you make the portions a little bigger, many of these small plates can serve as entrées as well.

Within each chapter, the recipes are roughly organized from light to heavy, from cold to hot, from small finger foods to more substantial fork-and-knife dishes.

the ingredients

It takes just as much time and effort to make a tomato salad with a good tomato as with a great one, but if you start with the great one, your finished dish will be that much more delicious. For that reason, I recommend using the best, highest quality ingredients you can find, and that your budget will allow.

I also recommend using ingredients in season. That's when fruits and vegetables will have the most flavor and be the best quality.

A few of the recipes involve seeking out an ingredient at a specialty food store, a good fishmonger or cheese shop, or a natural foods store. For those special and potentially unfamiliar ingredients, I've suggested where to find them and other ways to enjoy them, so that you'll have ample reason to use them up and, even better, use them again and again.

A lot of the recipes contain some form of acidity or brightness— lemon juice, vinegar, buttermilk, sour cream. This is because, in general, wine is pretty acidic, and so it helps marry food to wine if the food is also at least a little acidic. In fact, you'll be amazed at how often a little acid can turn a pretty good pairing into a great one.

Saltiness, too, can make a big difference in marrying a food to a wine. So you'll notice that in addition to calling for unsalted butter, as most recipes do these days, I also call for reduced-sodium broths. That's because saltiness can vary widely from brand to brand. Using salt-free or low-salt ingredients reduces the chance that one version of the finished dish will vary from another and, ultimately, puts you more in control of the outcome.

the salt

Because saltiness is so key to food and wine pairing, it's ideal if you use the same kind of coarse kosher salt that I do—Diamond Crystal kosher salt. It's cheap, it's available in every major supermarket, and it's what the pros use.

If, however, you prefer to use table salt, or any other finely ground salt, bear in mind that it has about twice the saltiness, by volume, as Diamond Crystal kosher salt. So use about half as much. The same goes for Morton's kosher salt.

VARIETALS: WINES BY ANOTHER NAME

In the United States, we label our wines varietally, or by the type of grape that was used to make the wine, like Sauvignon Blanc, Chardonnay, Pinot Noir, and Cabernet Sauvignon. And so the recipes in this book are divided by those varietal names.

In other parts of the world, though, wine might be labeled by where it's from. Burgundy from France, for example. To know what varietal that might be like, you have to know that in Burgundy, they grow mainly Chardonnay and Pinot Noir grapes. So a White Burgundy is essentially what we'd call a Chardonnay.

But you don't need to remember all that. The beginning of each chapter will include a list of other names that the varietal can go by.

---

a really brief discussion of food and wine pairing

(Warning: it's not important to understand any of this to enjoy the recipes in this book.) We've all heard a lot about how this wine tastes like strawberries and that one is buttery, and those nuances can come into play. But in pairing a wine to a food, the most important factors are the wine's broader characteristics, not the nuances. And those broad characteristics are:

- the wine's sweetness or dryness (lack of sweetness)
- the wine's acidity, crispness, or brightness
- the wine's tannins (which cause that bitter, dry-mouth feeling you often get from a red wine)
- the wine's weight or richness (how light or heavy it feels in your mouth)
- the wine's intensity (how subtle or strong its flavors are)

To create great food and wine combinations, the trick is to be familiar with these characteristics for each varietal—or at least the ones you like—and then apply a few very general tips about what works and what doesn't.

general pairing tips

■ 1. Pair sweet foods with sweet wines. *For example, chocolate and Port.* If you pair a sweet food with an unsweet, or dry, wine, it can make the wine taste sour or, in a red wine, it can accentuate those bitter, dry-mouth tannins. Even a dish that's just a little bit sweet, like honey-glazed ham or chicken with mango salsa, can have enough sweetness to make a dry wine taste less than ideal. So while sweet dishes need sweet wines, slightly sweet dishes often need slightly sweet, or off-dry, wines.

■ 2. Pair acidic foods with acidic wines. *For example, salad with a vinaigrette dressing and Sauvignon Blanc.* If you pair a not-very-acidic food with an acidic wine, it can make the wine taste more acidic, and sometimes downright sour.

■ 3. Pair rich/meaty/heavy, acidic, or slightly bitter foods with tannic wines (wines that give you that bitter, dry-mouth feeling you often get from a red wine). Adding salt will also help balance tannins. *For example, char-broiled steak with mustard sauce and Cabernet Sauvignon.* If you choose a food that fails to somehow account for the tannins in a wine, it can make the wine taste even more tannic, and sometimes unpalatably bitter.

It may seem strange to recommend adding bitterness to food, because we usually associate bitterness with unpleasantness. But there are many foods that have some bitterness, and that bitterness is enjoyable—a little charring on a grilled steak or a roasted red pepper, for example.

▓ 4. Pair light foods with light wines and heavy foods with heavy wines.

For example, tomato salad and Pinot Grigio, or Brie baked in puff pastry and Chardonnay. If you pair a light food with a heavy wine, or vice versa, things won't necessarily taste bad, they'll just seem out of balance. The heavier or richer component of the pairing will overwhelm the lighter one and sort of wash your experience of it away.

This tip is where you get the classic idea that white wine goes with fish and red wine goes with meat. And while that's a good rule of thumb, it's not always true. Salmon, for example, can pair beautifully with Pinot Noir—because salmon is heavy for a fish and Pinot Noir is light for a red wine.

▓ 5. Pair intense foods with intense wines.

For example, peppercorn steak and Syrah. As with the preceding tip, this helps prevent one component from overwhelming the other.

▓ 6. When considering a dish, consider its most expressive components.

For example, fillet of sole with cream sauce and Chardonnay. In other words, when deciding if your dish is sweet, acidic, rich/meaty/heavy, bitter, light, or intensely flavored, or some combination, don't look to its main ingredient. Consider the dish as a whole, identify the dominant flavors and textures, and then let those elements inform your wine choice.

In this example, the light fish might suggest a light wine. But the most expressive, or dominant, component of the dish isn't the fish—it's the cream sauce. And since that's rich, according to General Pairing Tip 4, the dish would be best with a rich wine, like Chardonnay.

fine-tuning tips

Once the basic principles are in play, if you like, you can do some fine-tuning. In fact, you'll notice that many of the recipes in this book suggest that you taste the final dish with your wine and adjust. That can really make the difference between a good combination and a perfect pairing.

■ 1. More salt or acid in the food will decrease the experience of acid and tannin, or that dry-mouth bitterness, and increase the experience of fruit or sweetness in the wine. *For example, if your food is making your wine taste sour, add salt or something acidic, like lemon or lime juice, vinegar, or buttermilk, to the recipe.* This is the adjustment that gets used most often because, in general, all wines are pretty acidic and red wines are pretty tannic. At the least, you want to hold up to those characteristics and, at the most, soften them.

■ 2. More sweet or savory elements in the food will increase the experience of acid and tannin, or bitterness, and decrease the experience of fruit or sweetness in a wine. *For example, if your food is making your wine taste too sweet or like it has lost its crispness, add something sweet, like fruit or honey, or something savory, like cured meats, aged cheese, or mushrooms, to the recipe.* More often than not, though, the problem will be too much sweetness or savory-ness in your food, increasing acid and tannins and decreasing the experience of fruit and sweetness in your wine. The way to remedy this is to add salt or acid to the food, per Fine-Tuning Tip 1, above, or switch to a sweeter wine, per General Pairing Tip 1.

■ 3. More rich or creamy elements in the food will help it pair with a rich or heavy wine. *For example, if your food is too light for your wine, add something rich or creamy, like butter, mayonnaise, avocado, or cream.*

■ 4. Wine in the food almost always helps wine go with the food. *For example, if you want to help a sauce, soup, or stew work with a wine, add some of that wine to the sauce, soup, or stew.* A small splash will help a little. A big pour will sometimes help a lot.

LEARN A LOT WITHOUT SPENDING A LOT: THROW A WINE-TASTING PARTY

Pick a varietal you want to know better and invite a few friends over. Ask each of them to bring a bottle of the varietal—it could be within a certain price range or you might want to try the varietal at different prices to see how cost affects its characteristics. Prepare a few recipes from this book that go with the wine you'll be tasting.

Once everyone arrives, open all the bottles and taste each wine, either as a group or individually. Notice each wine's overall characteristics—its sweetness (or lack thereof), acidity, tannins, weight, and intensity. Also make note of the wine's nuances, its flavors and aromas.

Once you've tasted four or six bottles, you'll start to get a sense of the varietal and what you can generally expect when you buy a bottle of it, any bottle of it.

After the initial tasting, bring in the food, enjoy it with the wine, and discuss what you've noticed. Repeat the party, perhaps rotating hosts, as often as you like, with as many varietals as you're interested in.

nuances

So far, we've been dealing solely with sweetness, acidity, tannins, weight, and intensity in food and wine. If all you paid attention to were those five factors, you'd have a near-perfect pairing every time.

Beyond those major flavor influences, though, there are nuances. Here's where the essence of strawberries and the buttery characteristics come into play. Some nuances tend to be characteristic of the varietal. For example, Sauvignon Blanc is known for having grassy or herbal characteristics. Once a food is working with Sauvignon Blanc on the basis of sweetness, acidity, tannins, weight, and intensity, you could add some herbs to the food, or ingredients that go well with herbs, like tomatoes, and it will be an even more perfect pair. If you want to make those adjustments, you'll find information about each varietal's nuances at the beginning of each chapter.

Some nuances tend to be characteristic of the way a particular producer makes a particular varietal, or characteristic of a particular growing region or vintage (year). If you know those particulars, you can work with them. If you don't, don't worry about it.

sauvignon blanc

One of the things that inspired me to write this book is that so many wines just don't taste good on their own—they need food to really help them sing.

To me, Sauvignon Blanc is one of those wines. I don't like it for sipping—it's just too acidic for me. But when you pair Sauvignon Blanc with food, especially food with a good amount of brightness, the wine gets softened and becomes a crisp, refreshing indulgence.

sauvignon blanc by another name

• *Bordeaux, White Bordeaux.* As with other French wines, these French Sauvignon Blancs are labeled with the name or area they're from. They might have the general area name Bordeaux, or names of subregions within Bordeaux (Graves, for example). Basically, any white wine from Bordeaux will be made from Sauvignon Blanc grapes, typically blended with some Sémillion. • *Sancerre, Pouilly-Fumé.* These names come from areas in France's Loire Valley, known for Sauvignon Blanc. • *Fumé Blanc.* Robert Mondavi is credited with coining this term, combining Sauvignon Blanc with Pouilly-Fumé. His winery still uses the name, and others have adopted it, too. Fumé Blancs often have some oak aging—that is, they're aged in contact with some form of oak—which can impart a lightly smoky quality.

pairing with sauvignon blanc

Although there are, of course, nuances to Sauvignon Blanc, the most important factors in food and wine pairing aren't a wine's nuances, but its broad strokes. If you learn a wine's overall characteristics and combine that information with the General Pairing Tips (page 6), you'll have a near-perfect pairing every time.

Broad characteristics:
• dry (not sweet)
• high in acidity, crispness, or brightness
• little or no tannins
• light to medium weight
• medium intensity

Pairs well with dishes that are:

- not sweet
- high in acidity, crispness, or brightness
- light to medium weight
- medium intensity

(Because the wine has little or no tannins, they're not a factor.)

For example, salad with vinaigrette dressing, sole with lemon-caper sauce, or vegetable soup with a splash of buttermilk.

fine-tuning

It's absolutely amazing how adding acidity will almost always help a Sauvignon Blanc pairing. Salt, too.

It's simply because the most dominant characteristic of Sauvignon Blanc is the acid. And so when pairing with this wine, per Fine-Tuning Tip 1 (page 8), you need to add generous amounts of salt and/or acid to stand up to that brightness.

Since Sauvignon Blanc is a light white wine, lighter, whiter acids like lemon juice, white wine or champagne vinegar, white or golden balsamic vinegar, buttermilk, and even sour cream work best. Very mild and refreshing spiciness can help add brightness as well, like the light tickle of a fresh radish, or a dash of hot sauce or horseradish.

Completely, and admittedly maddeningly, contrary to General Pairing Tip 4 (page 7), you can also sometimes use Sauvignon Blanc's high acidity to cut through bright but richer foods.

other nuances

Once you have a pairing that's working on the basis of sweetness, acidity, weight, and intensity, you can start playing with subtler nuances.

Some of the subtle flavors that you might find in a Sauvignon Blanc include grassiness, herbs, citrus (especially grapefruit), green apple, asparagus, bell pepper, a touch of smokiness (especially with Pouilly-Fumé and Fumé Blanc), and minerality. So it works to add those flavors, or foods that complement them, to your dishes.

other thoughts

Some foods that are considered classic pairings with Sauvignon Blanc are goat cheeses, fish and shellfish, chicken, salad with vinaigrette dressing, asparagus, tomatoes, and green vegetables.

minted pea bruschetta

This is a super-simple and really pretty dish, with a vivid green pea puree, rich brown walnut bread, and a white sour cream garnish.

If you want to make the presentation a little more restaurant-like, put the sour cream in a squeeze bottle and drizzle it over the toasts, Jackson Pollock-esque. • **MAKES 16 TOASTS**

1 cup fresh peas, blanched (see below), or frozen peas, thawed
24 fresh mint leaves
1½ teaspoons extra virgin olive oil
¾ teaspoon coarse kosher salt, or more to taste
Freshly ground black pepper to taste
16 small, thin slices walnut bread, or other dark or whole wheat
   artisan bread, toasted (see below)
⅓ cup sour cream

▓ In the bowl of a food processor, combine the peas, mint, olive oil, and salt and process to form a coarse puree, scraping down the bowl as necessary. (You can prepare the minted pea puree up to a day in advance, storing it covered in the refrigerator. If necessary, restir before proceeding.)

▓ Taste, ideally with your wine, and add pepper and/or more salt if you like. Spread each of the toasts with about 2 teaspoons of the puree. Top each with a 1-teaspoon dollop of sour cream and serve.

To blanch fresh peas: Cook the shelled fresh peas in boiling well-salted water (1 tablespoon of coarse kosher salt per quart) until tender, 1 to 2 minutes. Drain, then rinse in cold water until cool. (You can blanch the peas up to 2 days in advance, storing them covered in the refrigerator.)

To toast bread: Preheat the oven to 400°F. Place the bread slices on a baking sheet and bake until lightly browned, about 10 minutes, turning halfway through. (You can prepare the toasts up to a day in advance, storing them in an airtight container at room temperature.)

FOOD & WINE TIP The bruschetta might feel fancier garnished with crème fraîche, which is a type of sour cream. But besides being less expensive, regular sour cream is actually more sour, which helps marry it to the brightness of Sauvignon Blanc.

cheese puddle with orange olive oil and crushed red pepper

Bellwether Farms' Crescenza is a soft-ripened cheese that, at room temperature, becomes a buttery puddle, like the oozy insides of the triple-creamiest Brie you ever ate. You can buy Crescenza at better cheese shops or from www.bellwethercheese.com, or substitute a good triple-crème Brie, halved horizontally and splayed open.

I've riffed on this dish, using other, similarly oozy, creamy cheeses—and all were good. But Crescenza and Brie both have bright, almost sour notes that are best complemented by Sauvignon Blanc. I've also used herb-infused olive oil, and while that's good, too, the orange oil makes the sometimes tropical flavors of the wine pop. • SERVES 2 TO 4

One 6-ounce package Bellwether Farms Crescenza cheese (see above)
2 teaspoons orange olive oil, homemade (recipe follows) or store-bought
¼ to ½ teaspoon dried crushed red pepper flakes
1 baguette, cut on a diagonal into ½-inch slices

▦ Remove the cheese from its packaging and place it in the center of a platter or large plate. Set it aside for about an hour to come to room temperature.

▦ Just before serving, drizzle the orange olive oil over the cheese and sprinkle with the red pepper. Serve the baguette on the side for swiping up the cheese.

homemade orange olive oil • *Makes about ⅓ cup*

You can buy orange-infused olive oil at better supermarkets and specialty food stores. But it's easy and inexpensive to make, and a delicious ingredient to have on hand. Besides using it in this recipe, you can use it in salad dressings and drizzle it on grilled and roasted meats, poultry, and seafood.

½ cup extra virgin olive oil
Finely grated zest of 2 oranges (about 2 tablespoons packed)

In a small bowl, combine the olive oil and orange zest. Let the mixture stand at room temperature, stirring occasionally, for 2 hours. Strain through a fine-mesh sieve, pressing the solids. Discard the solids. (You can keep the orange olive oil for about a week, storing it covered in the refrigerator.)

prosciutto-wrapped asparagus with tarragon aïoli

Asparagus is said to be one of the hardest foods to pair with wine. That may be so, but the preparation and accessorizing of a dish are always more important in food and wine pairing than a single ingredient.

This dish is a perfect example. Because while the vegetal, green flavors of the asparagus might lean toward Sauvignon Blanc, the herbs and lemon in the aïoli seal the deal.

By the way, you can substitute other herbs for the tarragon, but keep them in the light, bright, springtime vein—like mint, cilantro, chives, or parsley—to keep them in sync with the wine.

• **MAKES 16 SPEARS**

16 asparagus spears
⅓ cup mayonnaise
1 tablespoon fresh lemon juice
2 teaspoons chopped fresh tarragon
2 cloves garlic, pressed through a garlic press or minced
6 thin slices prosciutto (about 3 ounces), cut crosswise in thirds
16 chives, 5 to 6 inches long

▓ Snap off the tough stem ends of the asparagus. In a large saucepan of boiling well-salted water (1 tablespoon of coarse kosher salt per quart), cook the asparagus until crisp-tender, 2 to 4 minutes, depending on the thickness of the asparagus. Drain, then rinse under cold water until cool. Transfer the asparagus to a paper towel-lined platter or plate and pat the spears dry.

▓ In a small bowl, combine the mayonnaise, lemon juice, tarragon, and garlic. Set aside. (You can prepare the asparagus and aïoli up to a day in advance, storing them covered in the refrigerator.)

▓ Wrap a piece of prosciutto around each asparagus spear. Tie the chives around the prosciutto. (You can prepare the wrapped asparagus up to 4 hours in advance, storing it covered in the refrigerator.)

▓ Arrange the asparagus on a platter or individual plates. Serve with the tarragon aïoli on the side for dipping.

FOOD & WINE TIP The tarragon aïoli would also be great alongside pan-fried petrale sole or poached salmon, and would also help marry those dishes to Sauvignon Blanc.

smoked trout salad with pumpernickel toasts

The hardest thing about making this dish is finding smoked trout, which should be pretty easy if you have a decent specialty food store in your midst. If not, you can substitute smoked salmon, but be sure it's smoked, not cured—in other words, use a dry, flaky, smoked fish, not a moist, thinly sliced fish like lox or gravlax.

In either case, the smoke is the complement to the wine, as is the slightly spicy watercress. Also, the crispness of the wine cuts through the richness of the fish. • **MAKES 16 TOASTS**

1½ cups loosely packed watercress leaves (about 1 ounce)
1 lemon
4 ounces smoked trout, skin removed, flaked
One 3-ounce package cream cheese, room temperature, cut into
    3 or 4 chunks
¼ to ½ teaspoon prepared horseradish
¼ teaspoon freshly ground black pepper, or more to taste
16 small, thin slices pumpernickel or dark rye bread, toasted
    (see page 13)

▓ Chop about half of the watercress and place in a medium bowl. Set the remaining whole leaves aside.

▓ Finely grate the zest from the lemon to yield 1 teaspoon packed. Juice the lemon to yield 2 tablespoons of juice. Add the zest and juice to the bowl with the watercress, along with the trout, cream cheese, horseradish, and pepper, stirring to make a spreadable paste. (You can prepare the trout salad up to 4 hours in advance, storing it covered in the refrigerator.)

▓ Taste, ideally with your wine, and add more lemon juice and/or pepper if you like. Spread about 1 tablespoon of the trout mixture on each of the toasts. Garnish with the reserved watercress and serve.

FOOD & WINE TIP Lighter smoky foods—like veggies or fish—go particularly well with Fumé Blanc, a kind of Sauvignon Blanc that often has a little oak aging, giving it a similarly woody, smoky quality.

spinach salad with edamame and pecorino

Sauvignon Blanc will always be a natural to pair with salads dressed with vinaigrette, the acidity of the dressing complementing the acidity of the wine. This recipe, especially nice in the winter or springtime, gets extra help with wine in the dressing and light, bright, springtime ingredients. • **SERVES 4**

2 tablespoons Sauvignon Blanc, or other dry white wine
1 tablespoon white wine vinegar or champagne vinegar
½ small shallot, minced
¼ teaspoon coarse kosher salt
Pinch freshly ground black pepper
3 tablespoons extra virgin olive oil
1 ounce pecorino cheese
9 cups loosely packed spinach (about 6 ounces), larger leaves torn into bite-sized pieces
½ cup shelled edamame (green soybeans), thawed if frozen
3 radishes, thinly sliced

▦ In a small bowl, combine the wine, vinegar, shallot, salt, and pepper, whisking until the salt dissolves. Whisk in the olive oil. Set aside. (You can prepare the dressing up to 3 days in advance, storing it covered in the refrigerator. Return to room temperature before serving.)

▦ Use a vegetable peeler to cut the cheese into thick shaves (you should have about ⅓ cup). Set aside. (You can shave the cheese up to a day in advance, storing it covered in the refrigerator.)

▦ In a large bowl, combine the spinach, edamame, radishes, and dressing to taste. Transfer the salad to a serving bowl or to individual plates, top with the cheese, and serve.

acidity: it's a good thing

You might think of acidity in food or wine as something unpleasant, like the mouth-puckering tartness you get if you bite into a lemon. But in moderation, acidity adds bright, high notes to foods and drinks. And it balances sweetness and richness to make both food and wine less cloying and more interesting.

Acidity also helps give a wine ageability, or the ability to improve with age. Another way to say that is, since acidity diminishes over time, a wine has to start with a good amount of it to maintain complexity and interest years later.

So don't think of acidity as a negative. Used appropriately, it can take foods and wines from blah to beee-youtiful.

celery root and scallion soup with croutons

Light and bright in taste and texture—and dead simple to make—this soup, along with a glass of Sauvignon Blanc, would be a perfect starter to a meal of broiled halibut or a big seafood salad.

Use smaller celery roots, also known as celeriac, because they'll be less woody than larger ones, and trim off all the dark brown spots. • **SERVES 6**

2 tablespoons unsalted butter
2 tablespoons extra virgin olive oil
4 small celery roots (celeriac) (about 2 pounds), well trimmed and cut into ½-inch dice (you should have about 3 cups)
1 russet potato, peeled and cut into ½-inch dice (you should have about 2 cups)
2½ teaspoons coarse kosher salt, or more to taste
Pinch white pepper, or more to taste
3½ cups reduced-sodium vegetable broth
10 scallions, white and light green parts only
1½ cups buttermilk
1 tablespoon fresh lemon juice, or more to taste
About ½ cup croutons, homemade or store-bought

▦ In a medium stockpot over medium heat, warm the butter and olive oil until the butter is melted. Add the celery root and cook, stirring occasionally, until it begins to brown, about 6 minutes. Stir in the potato, salt, and pepper and cook until the mixture is brown, about 4 minutes. Add the broth, scraping up any browned bits on the bottom of the pot. Bring to a boil, reduce to a simmer, and cook, stirring occasionally, until the vegetables are very soft, 6 to 8 minutes. Turn off the heat and let the liquid cool slightly.

▦ Meanwhile, slice 2 of the scallions very thin and set aside. Cut the remaining 8 scallions into rough ½-inch pieces.

▦ Working in batches, transfer the soup to a blender or food processor, add the ½-inch cut scallions, and puree, scraping down the jar or bowl as necessary. Return the mixture to the pot and stir in the buttermilk and lemon juice. (You can prepare the soup up to 3 days in advance. Cool it, then store it covered in the refrigerator.)

▦ If necessary, gently reheat the soup. Taste, ideally with your wine, and add more salt, pepper, and/or lemon juice if you like. Serve hot, garnished with the sliced scallions and croutons.

fresh corn with citrus butter

The simplicity of this dish belies its deliciousness, especially in the summer when corn is at its juicy best.

After your meal, repurpose any leftover citrus butter by storing it in the refrigerator or freezer. A pat or two on top of just-cooked fish or chicken makes for an easy sauce, and a dish that will pair well with either Sauvignon Blanc or Chardonnay. • SERVES 6

Finely grated zest of ½ orange (about 1½ teaspoons packed)
Finely grated zest of 1 lemon (about 1 teaspoon packed)
Finely grated zest of 1 lime (about 1 teaspoon packed)
1½ teaspoons coarse kosher salt, plus more for sprinkling
½ cup (1 stick) unsalted butter, room temperature
6 ears fresh corn, husked and cut in halves or thirds

▓ In the bowl of a food processor, combine the zests and salt and pulse to chop, scraping down the bowl as necessary. Add the butter, pulsing to combine, scraping down the bowl as necessary. Transfer the citrus butter to a small bowl or ramekin, or to individual very small bowls. (You can prepare the citrus butter in advance, storing it covered in the refrigerator for up to 3 days or in the freezer for several months. Thaw in the refrigerator before proceeding.)

▓ In a large pot of boiling well-salted water (1 tablespoon of coarse kosher salt per quart), cook the corn until crisp-tender, 3 to 5 minutes. Serve the corn warm, with the citrus butter and additional salt for sprinkling on the side.

FOOD & WINE TIP If you grill your corn instead of boiling it, the resulting roasty, toasty, caramelized flavors will pair better with Chardonnay.

chicken and endive salad sandwichettes

In addition to using it in sandwiches, you can pile the chicken salad mixture—which is especially pretty if you use both red and green Belgian endive—on top of a green salad or use it to fill a tomato half. Both dishes would also be perfect with Sauvignon Blanc.

In any case, the recipe is a great way to use up leftover chicken. Or plan ahead and cook an extra chicken breast along with your dinner a day or two before you plan to make the sandwichettes. Ideally, don't use rotisserie chicken. It has rich, roasty flavors that would be better suited to Chardonnay. • MAKES 6 SANDWICHETTES

¼ cup mayonnaise
1 tablespoon fresh lemon juice, or more to taste
½ teaspoon coarse kosher salt, or more to taste
⅛ teaspoon freshly ground black pepper, or more to taste
1 large cooked chicken breast, cut into ⅓-inch dice (you should have about 2 cups)
2 small heads Belgian endive, ideally 1 red and 1 green, cut crosswise into ¼-inch strips (you should have about 1 cup)
¼ cup chopped celery
2 tablespoons coarsely chopped fresh flat-leaf parsley
6 white or sourdough dinner rolls, split horizontally

▥ In a small bowl, combine the mayonnaise, lemon juice, salt, and pepper. In a medium bowl, combine the chicken, endive, celery, and parsley. Add the mayonnaise mixture to the chicken mixture, tossing gently. Taste, ideally with your wine, and add more lemon juice, salt, and/or pepper if you like.

▥ Arrange the bottom halves of the rolls on a work surface. Top with the chicken mixture, dividing it evenly, then cover with the top halves of the rolls. (You can prepare the sandwichettes up to 4 hours in advance, storing them covered in the refrigerator.)

▥ Cut the sandwichettes in half if you like, and serve.

pinot grigio

Pinot Grigio is one of the most popular white wines in Italy—and that's significant because the Italians really know about making wines to go with food. In the glass, with the wine on its own, you might not be wowed. But that sometimes lack of an in-your-face, distinctive character makes the wine more of a blank slate. And that's a good thing. The wine is easier to pair with a variety of foods because there's nothing you have to work around or account for.

For example, Pinot Grigio is similar to Sauvignon Blanc in that it's a crisp, lemony-lime, dry white wine. But it tends to be a little less acidic. So while some form of acid in the food almost always helps a food and wine pairing, the dishes that pair with Pinot Grigio can be softer. Also, Pinot Grigio can have a little more body than Sauvignon Blanc, lending it to slightly richer dishes.

All that said, the two wines are very similar. Many of the recipes in this chapter will work with Sauvignon Blanc, too.

pinot grigio by another name

• *Pinot Gris.* This is the name for the same grape in France, where it's widely grown in Alsace. Because the French don't label their wines by varietal, you're unlikely to see "Pinot Gris" on a French wine bottle, but a non-French producer might use the term, presumably to indicate the wine is made in a French style versus an Italian one.

pairing with pinot grigio

Although there are, of course, nuances to Pinot Grigio, the most important factors in food and wine pairing aren't a wine's nuances, but its broad strokes. If you learn a wine's overall characteristics and combine that information with the General Pairing Tips (page 6), you'll have a near-perfect pairing every time.

Broad characteristics:
• dry (not sweet)
• medium-high in acidity, crispness, or brightness
• little or no tannins
• light to medium weight
• medium intensity

Pairs well with dishes that are:

• not sweet
• medium-high in acidity, crispness, or brightness
• light to medium weight
• medium intensity

(Because the wine has little or no tannins, they're not a factor.)

For example, Italian antipasto, seafood pasta with white wine sauce, or salad with ranch or buttermilk dressing.

fine-tuning

As with Sauvignon Blanc, a little more acid and/or salt will almost always help a food pair with Pinot Grigio. Have some form of each on hand for fine-tuning dishes with your particular bottle.

And as with Sauvignon Blanc, because Pinot Grigio is a light white wine, use similarly lighter, whiter acids, like lemon juice, white wine or champagne vinegar, white or golden balsamic vinegar, buttermilk, and even sour cream. Sometimes simply adding some lemon zest or a bright cheese, like feta, will do the trick.

other nuances

Once you have a pairing that's working on the basis of sweetness, acidity, weight, and intensity, you can start playing with subtler nuances.

Some of the subtle flavors that you might find in a Pinot Grigio include citrus, green apple, pear, stone fruits, floral notes, and minerality. So it works to add those flavors, or foods that complement them, to your dishes.

Being the quintessential Italian white wine, Pinot Grigio also tends to work with lighter, typically northern Italian dishes and ingredients.

other thoughts

Some foods that are considered classic pairings with Pinot Grigio are goat and sheep cheeses, fish and shellfish, chicken, and pasta (especially with white sauces, wine sauces, and/or seafood).

baked goat cheese with herbed breadcrumbs

Chèvre, the fresh, creamy, spreadable cheese made from goat's milk, is a classic pairing with Sauvignon Blanc, and this recipe would work with that wine as well. • SERVES 4

1 tablespoon sherry vinegar
1 teaspoon coarse kosher salt
½ teaspoon freshly ground black pepper
¾ cup extra virgin olive oil, divided
1 cup panko (Japanese-style breadcrumbs)
2 teaspoons chopped fresh thyme
12 ounces chèvre (spreadable goat cheese)
6 cups loosely packed mixed salad greens (about 3 ounces)
2 tablespoons pine nuts, toasted (see below)

▓ In a small bowl, combine the vinegar, salt, and pepper, whisking to dissolve the salt. Whisk in 3 tablespoons of the olive oil. Set aside. (You can prepare the dressing up to 3 days in advance, storing it covered in the refrigerator. Return to room temperature before serving.)

▓ In a small, shallow bowl, combine the panko, thyme, and 1 tablespoon of the remaining olive oil. Place the remaining ½ cup of olive oil in another small bowl.

▓ Shape the chèvre into eight 1-inch-thick disks. Working with one disk at a time, dip both sides into the olive oil and then into the panko mixture, pressing gently on both sides and all edges so the crumbs adhere. Arrange the coated disk on a rimmed baking sheet. Place the baking sheet in the freezer for at least an hour. (You can freeze the cheese, covered, for up to 2 days.)

▓ Preheat the oven to 400°F.

▓ Transfer the baking sheet to the oven and bake until the panko is lightly golden, about 15 minutes.

▓ Meanwhile, in a large bowl, combine the greens and the dressing. Arrange the greens on a platter or on individual plates, dividing them evenly.

▓ Carefully arrange the baked cheese over the greens. Sprinkle with the pine nuts and serve.

To toast nuts: Preheat the oven to 350°F. Spread the nuts onto a rimmed baking sheet and bake until lightly browned and fragrant, 6 to 10 minutes, depending on the type of nut and the size of the pieces.

green apple caesar salad

With the rich flavors of Parmesan cheese and Caesar dressing, plus the bright crunch of apples and romaine lettuce, this salad is hearty and refreshing at the same time. • SERVES 4

1 ounce Parmesan cheese
1 head romaine lettuce, trimmed and cut or torn into bite-sized pieces (you should have 7 or 8 cups)
½ small tart green apple, such as Granny Smith or Pippin, cored and thinly sliced
½ small red onion, halved and thinly sliced
1 cup croutons, homemade or store-bought
½ cup Caesar salad dressing, homemade (recipe follows) or store-bought, or more to taste
Freshly ground black pepper, for serving

▓ Use a vegetable peeler to cut the cheese into thick shaves (you should have about ⅓ cup). (You can shave the cheese up to a day in advance, storing it covered in the refrigerator.)

▓ In a large bowl, combine the cheese, lettuce, apple, onion, croutons, and dressing. Serve immediately, passing the pepper grinder at the table.

homemade caesar salad dressing • *Makes ¾ cup*

¼ cup grated Parmesan cheese (about 1½ ounces)
¼ cup fresh lemon juice (from about 2 lemons)
2 cloves garlic
1½ teaspoons anchovy paste
1 teaspoon Dijon mustard
½ teaspoon Worcestershire sauce
½ teaspoon coarse kosher salt, or more to taste
½ teaspoon freshly ground black pepper, or more to taste
½ cup extra virgin olive oil

In a blender, combine the cheese, lemon juice, garlic, anchovy paste, mustard, Worcestershire, salt, and pepper and blend until smooth, scraping down the jar as necessary. With the motor running, slowly add the olive oil. Add more salt and/or pepper to taste. (You can prepare the dressing up to about a week in advance, storing it covered in the refrigerator. Return to room temperature and, if necessary, restir before using.)

FOOD & WINE TIP This dressing is particularly lemony. If you decide to use a bottled dressing instead, have a wedge or two of lemon at the ready, in case you need a squeeze on the salad to help balance the acidity in the wine.

heirloom tomato, mozzarella, and basil salad

This recipe is simple, easy, classic. A great example of how, when you use full-flavored, in-season ingredients, it doesn't take much to make a great-tasting dish.

Be aware, though, that tomatoes, especially heirlooms, can vary wildly in both sweetness and acidity, and if your tomatoes are too sweet, they can make the wine taste sour. So look for red and green heirlooms. In general, they'll have the highest acidity—not so much that they'll be sour, but enough to balance the sweetness— while yellow tomatoes will have the least. • **SERVES 4**

16 fresh basil leaves
4 large heirloom tomatoes (about 2 pounds), cored and cut into
   ¼-inch slices
Coarse kosher salt, to taste
Freshly ground black pepper, to taste
6 ounces fresh mozzarella cheese, cut into thin slices
2 tablespoons white or golden balsamic vinegar (see below)
2 tablespoons extra virgin olive oil
2 tablespoons minced red onion

▓ Cut 12 of the basil leaves into thin slices or tear them into small pieces. Set the remaining 4 leaves aside.

▓ Arrange the tomato slices on a platter or on individual plates, stacking them or fanning them out. Add a sprinkle of salt and pepper, a few pieces of the sliced or torn basil, and a slice of cheese between every one or two tomato slices.

▓ Drizzle the vinegar and olive oil over the tomatoes. Sprinkle with the onion, garnish with the reserved whole basil leaves, and serve.

NOTE You could say that white or golden balsamic vinegar is to balsamic vinegar as white grape juice is to grape juice—they're similar, but the white version is lighter and fruitier. White or golden balsamic is available at most major supermarkets and wherever regular balsamic is sold. Besides using it in this recipe, you can use it in Prosciutto Carpaccio with Asian Pears (page 63); Watercress Salad with Apricots and Almond-Crusted Brie, (page 79); and many of your favorite salad dressings.

FOOD & WINE TIP As is the case with many recipes in this chapter, this one would also pair well with Sauvignon Blanc.

tuna tartare with chive oil and pickled fennel

This recipe makes a tad more chive oil than you'll need, but that's a good thing, because you can use the extra in salads, drizzle it over just-grilled fish, or toss it with steamed potatoes. • SERVES 8

1 bunch chives, cut into rough ⅛-inch pieces (you should have about ¼ cup)
½ cup canola, grapeseed, or other neutral-flavored oil
¼ fennel bulb, halved lengthwise and sliced paper-thin
⅛ red onion, sliced paper-thin
⅓ cup white wine or champagne vinegar
1 pound sushi-grade tuna, finely diced
1 teaspoon coarse kosher salt, or more to taste
¼ teaspoon freshly ground black pepper, or more to taste
Toasts or crackers for serving, optional

▓ Set aside 2 teaspoons of the chives. In a food processor, combine the remaining chives with the oil and process for a few seconds, scraping down the bowl as necessary (it's not important to puree the chives, only to bruise them to help release their flavors). Let the mixture stand at room temperature, stirring occasionally, for 2 hours. Strain through a fine-mesh sieve, pressing the solids. Discard the solids. (You can prepare the chive oil up to a week in advance, storing it covered in the refrigerator.)

▓ In a medium bowl, combine the fennel, onion, and vinegar. Let stand at room temperature, stirring occasionally, for 2 hours. (You can prepare the pickled fennel up to 2 days in advance, storing it covered in the refrigerator. Return to room temperature before serving.)

▓ In a large bowl, combine ¼ cup of the chive oil with the tuna, salt, and pepper. Add more oil, salt, and/or pepper to taste.

▓ Drain the fennel mixture. Press about ⅛ of the tuna into a ¼ cup measuring cup. Overturn the measuring cup onto a plate. Top the tuna with about 1 tablespoon of the pickled fennel mixture. Drizzle a little of the remaining chive oil around the plate and garnish with some of the reserved chives. Repeat with the remaining tuna, pickled fennel, and chive oil. (You can plate the tartare up to an hour before serving, storing it covered in the refrigerator. You can refrigerate any remaining chive oil, covered, for up to about a week.)

▓ Serve the tartare with the toasts or crackers, if using.

lemony pasta carbonara with sugar snap peas

Pasta carbonara is one of my all-time favorite pastas—because it's so easy to make, yet so full of flavor. Basically, hot, just-cooked pasta is tossed with eggs, cheese, and crisped pancetta, making a flavorful, creamy-cheesy sauce.

Nine times out of ten, when cooking pasta, I'd say to use well-salted water, adding 1 tablespoon of coarse kosher salt per quart. That's pretty salty, but it really does take that much salt to get enough into the pasta to thoroughly season it. In this dish, though, there's already a good amount of salt in the pancetta and cheeses. So salt the pasta water only half as much. • **SERVES 6**

> One 4-ounce piece pancetta, cut into ¼-inch dice (you should have about 1 cup) (see note on page 64)
> 12 ounces orecchiette, or other pasta
> 8 ounces sugar snap peas, cut diagonally into ½-inch pieces (you should have about 2 cups)
> 4 large eggs
> ⅔ cup finely grated Parmesan cheese (3 to 4 ounces), plus more for serving
> ⅓ cup finely grated pecorino cheese (1½ to 2 ounces), plus more for serving
> 2 cloves garlic, pressed through a garlic press or minced
> Zest of 1 lemon, divided
> Freshly ground black pepper to taste

In a medium skillet over medium-low heat, cook the pancetta, stirring occasionally, until crisp, about 10 minutes. Use a slotted spoon to transfer the pancetta to a large bowl. Set aside to cool.

In large pot of boiling, mildly salted water (1½ teaspoons of coarse kosher salt per quart), cook the pasta according to package directions. Stir in the peas 2 minutes before the pasta is al dente.

While the pasta is cooking, add the eggs, cheeses, garlic, and half of the lemon zest to the bowl with the pancetta, whisking to combine.

Reserve ½ cup of the pasta cooking water. Drain the pasta. Immediately add the pasta and half of the reserved cooking water to the egg mixture, tossing to combine. Taste, ideally with your wine, and add pepper and/or more cooking water if you like. Serve hot, topped with the remaining lemon zest. Pass additional cheese at the table.

spring vegetable and prosciutto tart

This is a relatively simple yet delightfully special dish, thanks to the convenience of store-bought, always-elegant puff pastry.

You could make a case for pairing the tart with Sauvignon Blanc, and there'd be nothing wrong with that combination. But because of the weight of the dish—the rich pastry, the nutty Gruyère cheese, the potatoes—I prefer it with slightly weightier Pinot Grigio. • SERVES 4 TO 6

1 leek, white and light green parts only, cut into ¼-inch slices
3 small white or red potatoes (about 4 ounces), cut into ⅛-inch slices
1 sheet (half of a 17.3-ounce package) puff pastry, thawed
1¼ cups shredded Gruyère cheese (about 4 ounces), divided
4 ounces frozen artichoke hearts, thawed and quartered lengthwise (you should have almost 1 cup)
2 thin slices prosciutto (about 1 ounce), cut into ¼-inch strips
1½ teaspoons chopped fresh flat-leaf parsley
1½ teaspoons chopped fresh mint, tarragon, or a combination
1 lemon wedge

▦ Bring a medium saucepan of well-salted water (1 tablespoon of coarse kosher salt per quart) to a boil over medium-high heat. Add the leeks and cook until tender, 1 to 2 minutes. Remove the leeks with a slotted spoon and place on a paper towel-lined plate.

▦ Add the potatoes to the boiling water and cook until tender, 2 to 3 minutes. Drain. Set the potatoes and leeks aside. (You can prepare the leeks and potatoes up to 2 days in advance, storing them covered in the refrigerator. Return to room temperature before proceeding.)

▦ Line a baking sheet with parchment. On a floured surface, roll out the puff pastry to a 10-inch square. Transfer to the prepared baking sheet. Using a fork, pierce the pastry all over. Place the baking sheet in the refrigerator for at least 20 minutes. (You can refrigerate the pastry, covered, for up to a day.)

▦ Preheat the oven to 400°F.

▦ Sprinkle about ¾ cup of the cheese on the pastry, leaving a 1-inch border. Arrange the potatoes, leeks, artichokes, and prosciutto on top. Sprinkle with the remaining ½ cup of cheese. Bake the tart until golden, about 25 minutes.

▦ Just before serving, sprinkle the herbs and squeeze the lemon over the tart. Cut into pieces and serve warm or at room temperature.

grilled gouda sandwiches with apple compote

What's not to like about an ooey, gooey grilled cheese sandwich? This one is especially divine, thanks to a wonderfully melty, almost nutty cheese and an easy-to-make sweet-tart complement to spoon on top. • SERVES 4

1 lemon
¼ cup apple juice
1 tablespoon sugar
Pinch coarse kosher salt
1 tart green apple, such as Granny Smith or Pippin, peeled, cored, and cut into ½-inch dice
2 tablespoons unsalted butter, room temperature
6 slices French or sourdough bread
6 ounces Gouda cheese, thinly sliced

▓ Zest the lemon. Juice the lemon to yield 1 tablespoon of juice.

▓ In a medium saucepan over medium-high heat, combine the lemon zest, lemon juice, apple juice, sugar, and salt. Bring to a boil, stirring to dissolve the sugar and salt. Add the apple, return to a boil, and reduce to a simmer. Cover and cook, stirring occasionally, until the apple is tender, 7 to 8 minutes. Remove from the heat and set aside to cool. (You can prepare the apple compote up to 2 days in advance, storing it covered in the refrigerator. Return to room temperature before serving.)

▓ Spread the butter on one side of each piece of bread, dividing it evenly. Place 3 slices, buttered side down, on a work surface. Top with the cheese, dividing it evenly. Top with the remaining bread, buttered side up.

▓ Heat a large nonstick skillet over medium-low heat. Add the sandwiches, cover, and cook, in batches if necessary, until golden brown and the cheese is melted, 3 to 5 minutes per side. (You can also cook the sandwiches on a panini grill for 3 to 5 minutes.)

▓ Cut the sandwiches into quarters and serve hot, with the apple compote on the side.

FOOD & WINE TIP Be sure to use only a tart variety of apple for the compote. A sweeter apple will yield a sweeter compote, which could overpower the wine and make it taste sour.

baked shrimp with feta and wine

This is one of those dishes where the resulting juices are one of the best features. So serve it with plenty of warm, crusty bread for sopping up every last drop. • **SERVES 8**

2 tablespoons extra virgin olive oil
1 onion, cut into ½-inch dice
4 cloves garlic, thinly sliced
One 14½-ounce can diced tomatoes, drained
¾ cup Pinot Grigio, or other dry white wine
1 tablespoon chopped fresh oregano
¾ teaspoon coarse kosher salt
¼ teaspoon freshly ground black pepper
1½ pounds raw, peeled shrimp, preferably tail on
1 tablespoon chopped fresh flat-leaf parsley, divided
1 cup crumbled feta cheese (4 to 6 ounces)
Optional special equipment: eight 8-ounce gratin dishes or ramekins

▓ Preheat the oven to 375°F. Arrange a 2-quart casserole dish or eight 8-ounce gratin dishes or ramekins on a rimmed baking sheet.

▓ In a large skillet over medium-high heat, warm the oil. Add the onion and cook, stirring occasionally, until crisp-tender, 2 to 3 minutes. Add the garlic and cook, stirring occasionally, for 1 minute. Add the tomatoes, wine, oregano, salt, and pepper and bring to a boil. Remove the skillet from the heat and stir in the shrimp and 1½ teaspoons of the parsley.

▓ Transfer the mixture to the prepared casserole dish, gratins, or ramekins. Crumble the feta on top. Bake until the shrimp are cooked through and the cheese is slightly browned, about 15 minutes. Garnish with the remaining 1½ teaspoons of parsley and serve hot.

chardonnay

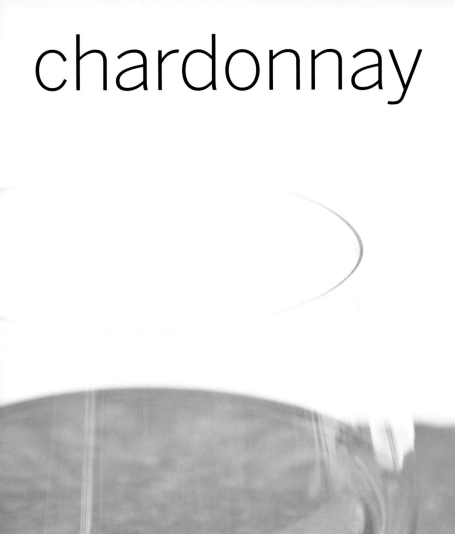

A lot of people drink only Chardonnay, which has led a lot of others to think it's overly popular and to eschew it. Personally, I couldn't do without Chardonnay in my food and wine pairing bag of tricks. Because as far as dry white wines go, Chardonnay is generally the biggest and weightiest of them all, and so is key to making pairings work with similarly rich, weighty foods.

Styles of Chardonnay can vary widely, from crisp and refreshing to buttery, sometimes oaky or toasty, and soft—and everything in between. When you pick up a bottle at the store, it's hard to know which kind you might be holding in your hand. If you have something in mind, talk to your retailer.

But my experience is that as long as you match Chardonnay's weight with richness in your food, it doesn't matter what style of Chardonnay you serve. The buttery ones will complement creamy flavors while the crisper ones will provide contrast and help cleanse your palate between bites.

chardonnay by another name

• *Burgundy, White Burgundy.* As with other French wines, these French Chardonnays are labeled with the name of the area they're from. They might have the general area name Burgundy, or names of subregions within Burgundy (Mâcon or Mâconnais, for example). Basically, any white wine from Burgundy will be made from the Chardonnay grape. • *Chablis.* Like Mâconnais, this is also an area in Burgundy, but one where they make Chardonnays with a characteristically crisp, steely, even mineral-y style.

pairing with chardonnay

Although there are, of course, nuances to Chardonnay, the most important factors in food and wine pairing aren't a wine's nuances, but its broad strokes. If you learn a wine's overall characteristics and combine that information with the General Pairing Tips (page 6), you'll have a near-perfect pairing every time

Broad characteristics:
• dry (not sweet)
• low to medium-high in acidity, crispness, or brightness
• little or no tannins
• medium to heavy weight
• medium to strong intensity

Pairs well with dishes that are:
- not sweet
- low to medium-high in acidity, crispness, or brightness
- medium to heavy weight
- medium to strong intensity

(Because the wine has little or no tannins, they're not a factor.)

For example, crackers and Brie, garlic roasted chicken, or French onion soup.

But overall, the most important factor in pairing foods to Chardonnay is the weight—pair rich foods with this rich wine.

fine-tuning

It seems like every single Chardonnay pairing is better with more cream, more mayonnaise, more cheese, more avocado.

If you know your Chardonnay is on the crisper side, your creamy elements can stand some acidity in them. For example, use buttermilk, sour cream, and even blue cheese.

If you know your Chardonnay is on the buttery side, keep your creamy elements blander. For example, use butter, mayonnaise, avocado, and buttery cheeses like Brie.

And if you don't know which kind of Chardonnay you've got, don't worry about it.

other nuances

Once you have a pairing that's working on the basis of sweetness, acidity, weight, and intensity, you can start playing with subtler nuances.

Some of the subtle flavors that you might find in a Chardonnay include apple, pear, stone fruits, tropical fruits, citrus, melon, toast, butterscotch, vanilla, nuts, and minerality. So it works to add those flavors, or foods that complement them, to your dishes.

other thoughts

Some foods that are considered classic pairings with Chardonnay are creamy cheeses, chicken (especially grilled or roasted), richer fish and shellfish (especially crab and lobster), veal, and anything with butter, cream, or a buttery/creamy sauce.

curried cashews

Spiced, roasted nuts, in different combinations of flavors and seasonings, are a great go-with for both wines and cocktails. But this version, bringing together the soft richness of cashews and the soft earthiness of curry powder to complement the crisp and soft flavors of Chardonnay, is just absolutely amazing.

If you're having a crowd or you just want more for munching, double the recipe (and cook it on two baking sheets).

• **MAKES ABOUT 4 CUPS**

1 egg white
4 cups roasted, salted cashews (about 1 pound)
⅓ cup sugar
1 tablespoon curry powder
1½ teaspoons coarse kosher salt

▨ Preheat the oven to 250°F.

▨ In a medium bowl, combine the egg white and 1 tablespoon of water, whisking until foamy. Add the cashews, tossing to coat. Transfer the cashews to a strainer, shake them, then let them drain for at least 2 minutes. Meanwhile, wipe out the bowl and add the sugar, curry powder, and salt, mixing to combine.

▨ Add the cashews to the sugar mixture, tossing to thoroughly and evenly coat.

▨ Spread the cashews onto a rimmed baking sheet in a single layer and bake for 40 minutes. Using a spatula, loosen the nuts from the baking sheet, stir them, and spread them out again. Reduce the oven temperature to 200°F and cook until the cashews are dry, about 30 minutes. Remove from the oven, loosen the cashews again, and set the pan on a wire rack to cool completely. (You can prepare the nuts up to a week in advance, storing them at room temperature in an airtight container.)

sweet potato garlic fries

You might wonder why this oven-baked French fry recipe uses sweet potatoes instead of regular russets. Either way, the fries will be easy, inexpensive, and delicious. But with yellow-fleshed sweet potatoes, sometimes called yams, they're just a little more sweet and creamy, which beautifully complements the wine. That said, don't use orange-fleshed sweet potatoes—they're too sweet.

Even though you might be able to squeeze all the potatoes onto one baking sheet, use two. More room around the fries helps them crisp up more easily. • **SERVES 3 OR 4**

2 yellow-fleshed sweet potatoes (about 1½ pounds), peeled
    if desired and cut into ¼ x ¼-inch sticks
¼ cup plus 1½ teaspoons canola, grapeseed, or other neutral-
    flavored oil, divided
2½ teaspoons coarse kosher salt, divided, or more to taste
4 cloves garlic, pressed through a garlic press or minced
1 teaspoon chopped fresh flat-leaf parsley, optional

▦ Preheat the oven to 450°F.

▦ In a large bowl, combine the potatoes with 3 tablespoons of the oil and 2 teaspoons of the salt, tossing to thoroughly and evenly coat. Arrange the potatoes on two large rimmed baking sheets in a single layer and bake for 15 minutes. Meanwhile, wipe out the bowl and set it aside.

▦ One pan at a time, remove the potatoes from the oven and toss them with a spatula. Rearrange the potatoes in a single layer and bake until crisp outside and cooked through, 12 to 15 minutes.

▦ Meanwhile, in a small microwavable bowl, combine the remaining 1 tablespoon plus 1½ teaspoons of oil and the garlic. Microwave on high for 30 seconds, until the garlic is tender.

▦ Transfer the potatoes back to the large bowl and toss with the garlic mixture, parsley, if using, and the remaining ½ teaspoon of salt. Taste, ideally with your wine, and add more salt if you like. Serve hot.

classic shrimp louis

This is absolutely heaven on a plate—a delectable combination of veggies, crunchy greens, creamy dressing, and a pile of sweet, succulent shrimp. The creaminess of the dressing makes it a natural for Chardonnay, and the touch of chili sauce in it helps bring out the fruit in the wine. If you like, substitute crab for the shrimp. Or do an indulgent combination of both. • **SERVES 6**

1 cup mayonnaise
1 tablespoon fresh lemon juice
1½ teaspoons chili sauce, such as Sriracha (see below)
1 teaspoon prepared horseradish
1 teaspoon coarse kosher salt
½ teaspoon Worcestershire sauce
2 heads butter lettuce, trimmed and separated into leaves or cut or torn into bite-sized pieces
1 carrot, shredded
1 pound cooked, peeled shrimp
3 hard-cooked eggs, peeled and quartered
1 avocado, peeled, pitted, and sliced
⅔ cup halved cherry tomatoes
2 scallions, white and light green parts only, thinly sliced on a diagonal

▦ In a small bowl, whisk together the mayonnaise, lemon juice, chili sauce, horseradish, salt, and Worcestershire. Set aside. (You can prepare the dressing up to 3 days in advance, storing it covered in the refrigerator.)

▦ Arrange the lettuce on individual plates, dividing it evenly. Sprinkle with the carrot, then arrange mounds of the shrimp, eggs, avocado, and cherry tomatoes on top, dividing them evenly. Spoon the mayonnaise mixture in the center, dividing it evenly. Sprinkle with the scallions and serve.

NOTE Sriracha is available in the ethnic or Asian section of most major supermarkets. Besides using it in this recipe, you can use it in Spicy Shrimp Sushi Rolls (page 74), in other dressings and sauces, and any time you want to add heat to your cooking.

FOOD & WINE TIP Chardonnay isn't the first wine I'd think of to pair with spicy food—that would probably be Riesling—but it can take a bit of heat as long as there's ample creaminess, as in this dressing.

chunky corn and avocado dip with pita toasts

For pairing with Chardonnay, this dish has it all. It's rich, fruity, bright, and buttery, just like the wine. Serve it in the summertime—at a picnic or by the pool—when fresh corn is at its peak.

• SERVES 10 TO 12

1 ear unshucked fresh corn
4 rounds pita bread
¼ cup (½ stick) unsalted butter, melted
4 ripe avocados (about 2 pounds), peeled and pitted
2 tablespoons fresh lime juice, or more to taste
2 tablespoons extra virgin olive oil
2 teaspoons coarse kosher salt, or more to taste
4 scallions, white and light green parts only, thinly sliced on a diagonal
Freshly ground black pepper to taste

▦ Preheat the oven to 375°F.

▦ Place the unshucked corn on a rimmed baking sheet and roast for 25 minutes, until the kernels are tender when pierced with a knife. Remove the corn and place it on a plate to cool. (You can prepare the corn up to a day in advance, storing it covered in the refrigerator.)

▦ If necessary, return the oven to 375°F.

▦ Cut the pitas in half. Split each half into two semicircles, then cut each semicircle into 4 wedges. Arrange the pita wedges on two baking sheets, smooth side down, and brush with the butter. Bake until lightly toasted, 10 to 12 minutes. Set aside to cool.

▦ Meanwhile, shuck the corn. Use a small, sharp knife to remove the kernels from the corn. Set aside.

▦ In a large bowl, use a potato masher or fork to combine the avocado, lime juice, olive oil, and salt. Add the corn kernels and scallions. Taste, ideally with your wine, and add more lime juice and/or salt or pepper if you like. Serve with the pita toasts on the side.

baked brie and roasted garlic in phyllo

Don't be daunted by the idea of working with phyllo! It's really quite easy, especially if you follow the tips in the note below. And you'll find phyllo is well worth the ever-so-slight effort—there's nothing like its delicately crisp and buttery layers, especially washed down with a sip of Chardonnay. • **SERVES 4**

15 cloves garlic
1 teaspoon extra virgin olive oil
1 teaspoon chopped fresh thyme
1/8 teaspoon coarse kosher salt
One 8-ounce round Brie cheese
4 tablespoons (1/2 stick) unsalted butter, melted
Four 14 x 18-inch sheets phyllo pastry, covered with a sheet of
    parchment or wax paper and then a damp kitchen towel (see below)
1/2 baguette, thinly sliced and toasted, optional (see page 13)

▦ Preheat the oven to 375°F.

▦ Place the garlic on an 8-inch square of foil, drizzle with the olive oil, and wrap the garlic in the foil, sealing the packet. Place the packet on a rimmed baking sheet and bake until the garlic is soft, 40 to 45 minutes. Carefully open the packet and set aside to cool. You can prepare the garlic up to a day in advance, storing it covered in the refrigerator.

▦ In a small bowl, mash the roasted garlic with the thyme and salt. Cut the Brie in half horizontally. Remove the top half, spread the garlic mixture on the bottom half, and replace the top. Set the Brie aside.

▦ Brush a rimmed baking sheet with some of the butter. Set aside.

▦ Transfer 1 sheet of phyllo to a work surface (keep the remaining phyllo covered) and brush it with some butter. Top it with 3 more sheets of phyllo, brushing each with butter.

▦ Use a sharp knife to trim the stack of phyllo into a 12-inch circle. Place the cheese in the center. Gently lift one edge of the phyllo circle up and over the cheese. Brush the folded pastry with butter. Continue to gently lift the phyllo in sections, folding each section snugly over the top of the cheese, brushing it with butter, and pressing it to adhere, until the cheese is wrapped. Place the wrapped cheese on the prepared baking sheet and refrigerate for at least 3 hours. (You can refrigerate the Brie, covered, for up to a day.)

▓ Preheat the oven to 400°F.

▓ Transfer the baking sheet to the oven and bake until the pastry is golden brown, about 25 minutes (if the cheese leaks from the pastry during baking, press a piece of foil over the tear in the pastry and continue baking). Cool 30 minutes, transfer to a platter, and serve warm, with the toasted baguette slices on the side, if using.

NOTE Sometimes phyllo can be brittle and crumbly, making laying out a sheet akin to putting together a jigsaw puzzle. But there are ways to avoid that problem. First, defrost your package of phyllo in the refrigerator overnight, not on the countertop the day you plan to use it. Defrosting it too quickly can make phyllo brittle. Second, don't refreeze phyllo, which can also make it brittle. Third, store any leftover phyllo in the refrigerator and use it within about a week. And fourth, know that no matter what you do, you'll occasionally get a bad sheet or even a bad box—so be willing to simply toss any less-than-perfect product.

FOOD & WINE TIP If you like your Chardonnay buttery, this ooey, gooey recipe will beautifully underline that rich, creamy flavor. If you like your Chardonnay crisp, the wine will nicely cut through the richness of the dish. If you don't know what kind of Chardonnay you like, don't worry about it. Any kind will work.

ham and brie baguettes

On the streets of Paris, vendors sell ham and Brie sandwiches like they sell hot dogs on the streets of New York. This version is jazzed up a bit with arugula and a mustard-mayo dressing, but even still, it evokes a French picnic. If you like, complete the scene by serving the sandwiches with White Burgundy, France's Chardonnay.

• SERVES 6

3 tablespoons Dijon mustard
2 tablespoons mayonnaise
1 baguette
8 ounces thinly sliced ham
4 ounces Brie cheese, cut into ¼-inch slices
4 cups loosely packed arugula (about 2 ounces)

▦ In a small bowl, combine the mustard and mayonnaise. Set aside. (You can prepare the dressing up to 3 days in advance, storing it covered in the refrigerator.)

▦ Trim the ends off the baguette. Cut crosswise into 4 lengths. Split each length horizontally, so it'll open like a book. Gently fold each piece open.

▦ Spread the mustard mixture on the bread, dividing it evenly. Arrange the ham, cheese, and arugula on top, dividing them evenly. (You can prepare the sandwiches up to 4 hours in advance, storing them covered in the refrigerator.)

▦ Press the bread tops down lightly, cut each sandwich in thirds, and serve.

FOOD & WINE TIP To pair this sandwich with Sauvignon Blanc, omit the mayonnaise and double the Dijon. To pair it with Riesling, make the dressing with 4 tablespoons of Dijon and 2 tablespoons of honey.

roasted red potatoes with sage butter

This dish makes a wonderful side for roast chicken or fish, or combine it with other dishes in this chapter for an all-Chardonnay small plates meal.

You'll likely have leftover sage butter—just freeze or refrigerate it. Then use a pat or two on top of a just-grilled chicken breast or pork chop, or toss some into sautéed vegetables. All those dishes will pair with Chardonnay as well. • SERVES 4

36 fresh sage leaves
1 tablespoon coarse kosher salt, divided, or more to taste
6 tablespoons (¾ stick) unsalted butter, room temperature
16 small red potatoes (about 1½ pounds)
2 tablespoons extra virgin olive oil

▓ Preheat the oven to 450°F.

▓ In the bowl of a food processor, combine the sage and 1½ teaspoons of the salt and pulse to coarsely chop, scraping down the bowl as necessary. Add the butter and pulse to combine, scraping down the bowl as necessary. (You can prepare the sage butter in advance, storing it covered in the refrigerator for up to a day or in the freezer for about a month. Return to room temperature before serving.)

▓ In a large bowl, combine the potatoes, olive oil, and the remaining 1½ teaspoons of salt, tossing to thoroughly and evenly coat. Arrange the potatoes on a rimmed baking sheet and bake until browned and tender, about 30 minutes, tossing halfway through. Meanwhile, wipe out the bowl and set it aside.

▓ Transfer the potatoes back to the bowl and toss with the sage butter to taste. Taste, ideally with your wine, and add more salt if you like. Serve hot.

FOOD & WINE TIP This recipe is a good example of a counterintuitive food and wine pairing rule: the main ingredient isn't the main thing to consider. What's most important is a dish's most expressive component. Here, the potatoes aren't much of a factor because they don't have much flavor. The sage butter that accessorizes them, though—that's what calls for Chardonnay.

dungeness crab cakes with meyer lemon mayo

A Meyer lemon is a beautiful cross between a standard, or Eureka, lemon and a mandarin orange. It has delicious lemon flavor, but with more sweetness—and minus the acidic ouch that a lemon can have. The Meyer also reflects a lovely floral quality from the mandarin. It's a wonderful, wonderful ingredient to cook with.

That said, unlike most citrus fruits, the Meyer isn't always available. If it's out of season or you can't find it, you can get pretty close by combining a standard lemon with, of course, a mandarin. If mandarins are out of season, too, use a naval orange.

Any and all combinations of lemons and oranges will taste great.

• SERVES 4

2 Meyer lemons, or 2 standard lemons and 1 mandarin or navel orange
⅔ cup mayonnaise
3 tablespoons extra virgin olive oil, divided
4 shallots, finely diced
3 large eggs
1 cup panko (Japanese-style breadcrumbs)
¼ cup chopped fresh flat-leaf parsley
1½ teaspoons coarse kosher salt
½ teaspoon freshly ground black pepper
12 ounces cooked Dungeness crabmeat, picked over (see below)
4 large butter lettuce leaves
2 tablespoons unsalted butter

▥ Zest 1 of the Meyer lemons. Juice the zested lemon to yield 1 tablespoon of juice. (If using standard lemons and a mandarin or orange, zest half of 1 lemon and ¼ of the mandarin or orange. Juice each to yield 1½ teaspoons of juice.) In a small bowl, combine the zest, juice, and mayonnaise. Set aside. Cut the remaining lemon into 8 wedges. Set aside. (You can prepare the Meyer lemon mayo and lemon wedges up to 3 days in advance, storing them covered in the refrigerator.)

▥ In a small skillet over medium heat, warm 1 tablespoon of the olive oil. Add the shallots and cook, stirring occasionally, until tender, about 1 minute. Remove from the heat, transfer to a large mixing bowl, and set aside to cool.

Add the eggs, panko, parsley, salt, and pepper to the cooled shallots, whisking to combine. Gently mix in the crab. Shape the mixture into 8 cakes, about 2 inches in diameter and ¾ inch thick. (You can shape the crab cakes up to a day in advance, storing them covered in the refrigerator.)

Arrange the lettuce leaves and lemon wedges on a platter or on individual plates, dividing them evenly. Set aside.

In a large skillet on medium heat, melt the butter and the remaining 2 tablespoons of olive oil. Carefully add the cakes and cook until golden brown, 2 to 3 minutes per side.

Arrange the cakes on top of the lettuce leaves. Top with a dollop of the mayonnaise mixture and serve hot.

NOTE Dungeness is a Pacific crab, found from Alaska to Mexico. If it's not in season or not available where you live, or if you have a different local catch, substitute another crab. In a pinch, you can even use canned crab.

FOOD & WINE TIP This recipe is also great with Viognier.

french onion soup

There is a restaurant in Napa called Angèle, and during the winter months my husband and I love to occasionally treat ourselves to a midweek lunch there, cozying up to a bowl of French onion soup with a glass of Chardonnay on the side. The combination is heavenly—but it certainly doesn't hurt that it's a charming French bistro, or that my charming husband is sitting there with me.

This soup will make you, too, feel like you're in a charming French bistro. • **SERVES 6**

4 tablespoons (½ stick) unsalted butter
4 onions (about 2 pounds), halved lengthwise and thinly sliced
2 sprigs fresh thyme
2 bay leaves
2 teaspoons coarse kosher salt
1 teaspoon freshly ground black pepper
1 tablespoon all-purpose flour
2 cups Chardonnay, or other dry white wine
4 cups reduced-sodium beef broth
Six ¾-inch-thick slices crusty artisan French bread
2 tablespoons cognac or brandy
6 ounces Gruyère cheese, thinly sliced
Optional special equipment: six 10-ounce ovenproof crocks or bowls

▓ In a medium stockpot over medium heat, melt the butter. Add the onions, thyme, bay leaves, salt, and pepper and cook, stirring occasionally, until the onions are soft, about 10 minutes. Reduce the heat to low and cook, stirring occasionally, until the onions are golden, 45 minutes to 1 hour. (If the onions are still pale after 45 minutes, increase the heat slightly.) Sprinkle in the flour and cook, stirring, for 1 minute. Stir in the wine and cook, stirring, for 1 minute. Stir in the broth, bring to a boil over high heat, reduce to a simmer, and cook, stirring occasionally, for 30 minutes.

▓ Meanwhile, preheat the oven to 350°F.

▓ Cut the bread slices to fit on top of 10-ounce ovenproof crocks or bowls. (If you don't have 10-ounce ovenproof crocks or bowls, leave the slices whole.) Arrange the bread in one layer on a large rimmed baking sheet and bake until dry, about 15 minutes, turning halfway through. Let the bread cool on the baking sheet until about 5 minutes before you're ready to serve. (You can prepare the soup and dry the bread up to 3 days in advance. Cool the soup, then store it covered in

(continued on next page)

the refrigerator. Cool the bread, then store it in an airtight container at room temperature. Gently reheat the soup before proceeding.)

▦ Preheat a broiler. Arrange six 10-ounce ovenproof crocks or bowls, if using, on a rimmed baking sheet. Arrange an oven rack so that the rims of the bowls will be 4 or 5 inches from the heat.

▦ Remove the thyme stems and bay leaves from the soup and stir in the brandy. Ladle the soup into the crocks and top with the toasts. Arrange the cheese on top, covering the toasts and letting the cheese hang over the rims of the crocks. Broil 4 or 5 inches from the heat until the cheese is melted and bubbly, 2 to 3 minutes. (If you don't have ovenproof crocks or bowls, leave the toasts on the baking sheet, top with the cheese, and broil 4 to 5 inches from the heat until the cheese is melted and bubbly. Meanwhile, ladle the soup into bowls. Top the soup with the cheesy toasts.)

▦ Serve immediately, warning your guests that the bowls are very hot.

fruit: proceed with caution

You might think that since there are fruit flavors in wine, you can enhance a food and wine pairing by adding fruit to the food. In theory, that's a good idea. But in practice, since most fruit is sweet, adding it can accentuate the acidity and/or the bitter tannins in the wine, per Fine-Tuning Tip 2 (page 8).

Sometimes you can compensate for this by making sure there's enough acid in the food. Or you can use a tart fruit, like a green apple. Or you can add fruity flavors without adding fruit per se—for example, an orange-infused olive oil. If none of those tricks are working and your food is still making your wine taste sour or bitter, switch to an off-dry, or slightly sweet, wine, such as an off-dry Riesling, Gewürztraminer, or Rosé.

caramelized onion, blue cheese, and rosemary pizza

Caramelized onions are one of the world's most simple yet delicious ingredients, with unctuous, creamy-sweet qualities that will almost always help a dish pair well with Chardonnay.

It's no big trick to make caramelized onions. It just takes patience—slow, gentle cooking will yield melt-in-your-mouth wonderfulness, while haste will make charred, blackened horribleness.

And a few words about blue cheese, which also has a nice affinity to Chardonnay. It can range in saltiness. If you notice your wine is tasting a little acidic, or sour, your cheese is probably not very salty. Just sprinkle a little salt on the pizza and the wine should lose its bite. • SERVES 4 TO 8

4 tablespoons (½ stick) unsalted butter
2 onions (about 1 pound), halved and cut into ¼-inch strips
1½ teaspoons coarse kosher salt
½ teaspoon freshly ground black pepper
One 12-ounce pizza dough, homemade or store-bought
¾ cup crumbled blue cheese (about 3 ounces)
1 tablespoon chopped fresh rosemary
2 tablespoons chopped hazelnuts, toasted, optional (see page 26)

▦ In a large skillet over medium heat, melt the butter. Add the onions, salt, and pepper and cook, stirring occasionally, until soft, about 5 minutes. Reduce the heat to very low and cook, stirring occasionally, until the onions are golden, 30 to 45 minutes. Set aside to cool. (You can prepare the caramelized onions in advance, storing them covered in the refrigerator for up to 3 days or in the freezer for several months. Return to room temperature before proceeding.)

▦ Preheat the oven, along with a pizza stone if you have one, to 500°F.

▦ On a lightly floured work surface, roll or stretch the dough out to a 12- to 14-inch round. Transfer the dough to a pizza pan or a flour- or cornmeal-dusted pizza paddle. Top with the caramelized onions, cheese, and rosemary. Transfer the pizza to the oven and bake for 10 to 12 minutes, until the pizza is golden and crisp.

▦ Sprinkle the pizza with the hazelnuts, if using, cut into wedges, and serve hot.

viognier

've saved the Viognier, Riesling, and Gewürztraminer chapters for the end of the white wine section because I think they're wines that you might be less familiar with—but they're worth getting to know.

Viognier (vee-ohn-YAY) is undoubtedly an up-and-comer, increasingly showing up in both cult wine shops and supermarkets, in all price categories.

Like Chardonnay, Viognier is relatively full-bodied, and so it works well with many of the same rich dishes. It also has flavors of stone fruits and pears, although sometimes the fruits can be more pronounced, sometimes giving the impression of sweetness even though the wine is dry.

My favorite thing about Viognier, though, is its beautiful floral quality, a quality that opens the door to pairing it with foods that have similarly exotic and aromatic characteristics and even some ethnic cuisines. On the down side, Viognier can be very mineral-y, almost steely, which can sometimes make pairings challenging.

viognier by another name

• *Condrieu.* This name comes from the area in France's Rhône Valley known for Viognier.

pairing with viognier

Although there are, of course, nuances to Viognier, the most important factors in food and wine pairing aren't a wine's nuances, but its broad strokes. If you learn a wine's overall characteristics and combine that information with the General Pairing Tips (page 6), you'll have a near-perfect pairing every time.

Broad characteristics:
• dry (not sweet)
• medium-low to medium in acidity, crispness, or brightness
• little or no tannins
• medium to heavy weight
• medium to strong intensity

Pairs well with dishes that are:
• not sweet
• medium-low to medium in acidity, crispness, or brightness

- medium to heavy weight
- medium to strong intensity

(Because the wine has little or no tannins, they're not a factor.)

For example, chicken curry, macadamia-crusted halibut, or roasted root vegetables.

fine-tuning

The kinds of foods that pair well with Viognier are very similar to those that pair well with Chardonnay. And as with Chardonnay, you can almost never go wrong adding more richness to a Viognier dish. Try cream, butter, mayonnaise, soft cheeses, and even toasted nuts.

But be careful with acidity or bitterness if you want a dish to work with Viognier—too much can wash out the fruit and accentuate the steely, austere quality that the wine can have.

other nuances

Once you have a pairing that's working on the basis of sweetness, acidity, weight, and intensity, you can start playing with subtler nuances.

Some of the subtle flavors that you might find in a Viognier include stone fruits, pear, citrus, baking spices, floral notes, and minerality. So it works to add those flavors, or foods that complement them, to your dishes.

other thoughts

Some foods that are considered classic pairings with Viognier are creamy cheeses, chicken (especially roasted), richer fish and shellfish (especially crab and lobster), curries, toasted nuts, pork, and anything with butter, cream, or a buttery/creamy sauce.

nutty fondue

Is there anything better than a pot full of melted cheese begging to be dipped into? If so, it has to be melted cheese with wine and toasted nuts mixed in. The simplicity of its ingredients and its ease of preparation belie this fondue's sinful deliciousness.

If you can't find walnut bread to serve alongside the fondue, use any kind of crusty artisan bread. • SERVES 6

One 1-pound loaf walnut bread, or other artisan bread, cut into
   1-inch cubes
5 cups shredded Gruyère cheese (about 1 pound)
2 tablespoons all-purpose flour
2 tablespoons chopped almonds, toasted (see page 26)
2 tablespoons chopped hazelnuts, toasted (see page 26)
2 tablespoons chopped macadamia nuts, toasted (see page 26)
1 cup Viognier, or other dry white wine
2 tablespoons kirsch, optional
Optional special equipment: fondue pot and fondue forks

▓ Preheat the oven to 375°F.

▓ Place the bread on two rimmed baking sheets and bake until very lightly toasted on the outside but still soft in the middle, about 8 minutes. Set aside to cool slightly or completely.

▓ In a medium bowl, toss the cheese with the flour. In a small bowl, combine the nuts. Set both bowls aside. (You can prepare the bread, flour, and nuts up to 4 hours in advance, storing them loosely covered at room temperature.)

▓ In a fondue pot or medium saucepan over medium-high heat, bring the wine to a simmer. Lower the heat to medium-low and stir in the cheese mixture, about ½ cup at a time, adding more when the previous addition has melted.

▓ Set aside about 1 tablespoon of the nuts. Stir the remaining nuts and the kirsch, if using, into the cheese mixture. If not using a fondue pot, transfer the mixture to a serving bowl. Sprinkle the reserved nuts on top and serve hot, with the toasted bread on the side for spearing and dipping.

FOOD & WINE TIP Wine in the food helps a wine go with the food, but you don't have to use a particular varietal to accomplish the task. In other words, it's important to use white wine when a recipe calls for white, red wine when a recipe calls for red, dry wine (as opposed to sweet) when a recipe calls for dry, and sweet wine when a recipe calls for sweet. Other than that, it doesn't hurt to use the same varietal that you'll be serving, but it's not critical.

hazelnut shrimp salad in butter lettuce cups

This salad gets its Viognier-friendly hazelnut flavor from two sources, toasted hazelnuts and hazelnut oil. Hazelnut oil can be found at specialty food stores and better supermarkets. And it's worth seeking out—besides being a key ingredient in this recipe, it'll add deliciously nutty flavor to all kinds of salads, soups, stews, and pastas. You can even use a little in your baking to give muffins, cookies, and cakes a roasty, toasty something special. But if you can't find it or would rather not spend the money on it, don't stress. Just substitute another nut oil or a neutral-flavored oil.

Another element that helps with the pairing is the avocado. I've served this dish many times without it, but that added creaminess really makes the salad perfect for the wine. • **SERVES 4**

6 tablespoons hazelnut oil (see above)
Zest of 1 lemon
1 clove garlic, pressed through a garlic press or minced
1 teaspoon coarse kosher salt, or more to taste
¼ teaspoon white pepper, or more to taste
1 head butter lettuce
12 ounces cooked peeled shrimp, coarsely chopped if larger than very small
1 avocado, peeled, pitted, and cut into ¼-inch dice
¼ cup chopped fresh chives
3 tablespoons chopped hazelnuts, toasted, divided (see page 26)

░ In a small bowl, combine the hazelnut oil, lemon zest, garlic, salt, and pepper, whisking to dissolve the salt. Set aside. (You can prepare the dressing up to 3 days in advance, storing it covered in the refrigerator.)

░ Remove 8 large leaves from the head of lettuce. Arrange them on a platter or on individual plates, dividing them evenly. Coarsely chop the remaining lettuce and place it in a large bowl. Add the shrimp, avocado, chives, 2 tablespoons of the hazelnuts, and the dressing, gently tossing to combine. Taste, ideally with your wine, and add more salt and/or pepper if you like.

░ Arrange the shrimp mixture on top of the lettuce leaves. Sprinkle with the remaining 1 tablespoon of hazelnuts and serve.

lobster claw slaw

Here, crunchy, creamy, deliciously familiar slaw is sumptuously
chock full of rich, succulent lobster meat—for a dish that would
be just as at home at a beach bash as at an elegant dinner party. For
occasions that might not merit the indulgence of lobster, feel free
to substitute shrimp or crab. • SERVES 8

½ cup mayonnaise
2 tablespoons sour cream
2 tablespoons whipping cream
¼ teaspoon white pepper, or more to taste
2 tablespoons plus ½ teaspoon coarse kosher salt, divided, or more
   to taste
One 10-ounce bag finely shredded cabbage or slaw mix
3 cups loosely packed arugula (1½ ounces)
½ small head radicchio, cored and thinly shredded (you should have
   about 1¾ cups)
1 shallot, halved lengthwise and thinly sliced
1 tablespoon chopped fresh tarragon, plus sprigs for garnish
12 ounces cooked lobster meat, cut or shredded into bite-sized pieces
8 large or 16 small cooked lobster claws

▦ In a small bowl, combine the mayonnaise, sour cream, cream,
pepper, and ½ teaspoon of the salt. Set aside. (You can prepare the
mayonnaise mixture up to 3 days in advance, storing it covered in the
refrigerator.)

▦ In a large bowl, combine the remaining 2 tablespoons of salt and 2
cups of cold water, whisking to dissolve the salt. Add the cabbage and,
if necessary, enough additional water to cover. Soak for an hour, stirring
occasionally. (If you're pressed for time, you can skip this step—it helps
make the slaw more crisp and crunchy, but it's not critical.)

▦ Drain the cabbage and return it to the bowl. Add the arugula,
radicchio, shallot, and chopped tarragon. Gently stir in the lobster. Add
the mayonnaise mixture, gently tossing to combine. Taste, ideally with
your wine, and add more salt and/or pepper if you like.

▦ Arrange the lobster slaw on a platter or on individual plates, dividing it evenly. Top with the lobster claws and tarragon sprigs and serve.

FOOD & WINE TIP As with many of the recipes in this chapter, this one would
also pair well with Chardonnay.

five-spice crab salad cocktails

If you're looking for something elegant, look no further. This cocktail is super-simple to make, but because it features an indulgent ingredient, crab, it feels sophisticated and special-occasion. Ideally, use fresh crab from a good fishmonger, but canned crab will work as well.

The dish is great on its own, but with the wine, it's a knockout—one of those delicious situations where the whole is greater than the sum of its parts. • **SERVES 4**

½ cup mayonnaise
2 teaspoons fresh lemon juice, or more to taste
½ teaspoon Chinese five-spice powder, plus more for garnish (see below)
12 ounces cooked crabmeat, picked over
¼ cup chopped fresh flat-leaf parsley, plus leaves for garnish
2 tablespoons minced shallot

▓ In a small bowl, combine the mayonnaise, lemon juice, and five-spice powder. Set aside. (You can prepare the mayonnaise mixture up to 3 days in advance, storing it covered in the refrigerator.)

▓ In a medium bowl, combine the crab, chopped parsley, and shallot. Add about 2 tablespoons of the mayonnaise mixture, gently tossing to combine. Taste, ideally with your wine, and add more lemon juice if you like.

▓ Spoon the crab mixture into decorative glasses. Top with the remaining mayonnaise mixture, dividing it evenly. Sprinkle with a dash of five-spice powder, garnish with the parsley leaves, and serve.

NOTE Chinese five-spice powder is available in either the spice section or the ethnic or Asian section of most major supermarkets. Besides using it in this recipe, you can use it in Tea-Smoked Sturgeon (page 82), sprinkle it on roasted meats and vegetables, and stir it into rice.

FOOD & WINE TIP With a teaspoon of lemon zest instead of the five-spice powder, this dish is great with Chardonnay.

prosciutto carpaccio with asian pears

As you can probably tell by its liberal use throughout these recipes, salty, savory prosciutto is an ideal accompaniment to many wines. Here, it's combined with a mayonnaise-based sauce, nutty arugula, and fragrant Asian pears to make an ideal accompaniment to rich, floral Viognier.

If you want to make the presentation a little more restaurant-like, put the mayonnaise mixture in a squeeze bottle and drizzle it over the prosciutto, Jackson Pollock-esque. • SERVES 4

3 tablespoons mayonnaise
1 tablespoon Dijon mustard
¼ teaspoon ground cloves
1½ teaspoons extra virgin olive oil
1½ teaspoons white or golden balsamic vinegar (see note on page 29)
⅛ teaspoon coarse kosher salt
Pinch freshly ground black pepper
½ Asian pear, cored and cut into ¼-inch dice
12 thin slices prosciutto (about 6 ounces)
2 cups loosely packed arugula (about 1 ounce)

▧ In a small bowl, combine the mayonnaise, mustard, and cloves. Set aside.

▧ In medium bowl, combine the olive oil, vinegar, salt, and pepper, whisking to dissolve the salt. Set aside. (You can prepare the mayonnaise sauce and the dressing up to 3 days in advance, storing them covered in the refrigerator.)

▧ Add the pear to the dressing, tossing to combine.

▧ Arrange the prosciutto slices, slightly overlapping, on individual plates, dividing them evenly. Drizzle on the mayonnaise mixture, dividing it evenly. Mound some arugula in the center of each plate, sprinkle with the pear mixture, and serve.

pumpkin and pancetta soup

The hardest thing about making this soup is tackling the pumpkin—and that's not very hard at all. Just use a sharp knife to cut it into quarters, use a large spoon to scrape the seeds out of each piece, then use a vegetable peeler to remove the peel. If the pumpkin is proving difficult to quarter, pierce it a few times, then microwave it for a couple of minutes, which will soften it up. • SERVES 6

One 8-ounce piece pancetta, cut into ¼-inch dice (you should have about 2 cups) (see below)
One 2½-pound sugarpie pumpkin, other cooking pumpkin, or butternut squash, seeded, peeled, and cut into ½-inch dice (you should have about 6 cups)
1 teaspoon coarse kosher salt, or more to taste
½ teaspoon freshly ground black pepper, or more to taste
2 tablespoons chopped fresh sage leaves, divided
4 cups reduced-sodium chicken broth
½ cup whipping cream

▦ In a medium stockpot over medium heat, cook the pancetta, stirring occasionally, until crisp, 6 to 8 minutes. Use a slotted spoon to transfer the pancetta to a paper towel-lined plate.

▦ Increase the heat to medium-high and add the pumpkin, salt, pepper, and 1½ tablespoons of the sage. Cook, stirring occasionally, until the pumpkin is brown and crisp-tender, 8 to 10 minutes. Add the broth, scraping up any browned bits on the bottom of the pot. Bring to a boil, reduce to a simmer, and cook, stirring occasionally, until the pumpkin is very soft, 6 to 8 minutes. Turn off the heat and let the liquid cool slightly.

▦ Working in batches, transfer the soup to a blender or food processor, add about half of the pancetta, and puree, scraping down the jar or bowl as necessary. Return the mixture to the pot and stir in the cream. (You can prepare the soup up to 3 days in advance. Cool it, then store it covered in the refrigerator.)

▦ If necessary, gently reheat the soup. Taste, ideally with your wine, and add more salt and/or pepper if you like. Serve hot, garnished with the remaining pancetta and the remaining 1½ teaspoons of sage.

NOTE Pancetta is an Italian bacon that comes shaped into a sliceable, sausage-like roll. Because it's not smoked, it has a slightly different flavor than American bacon. Pancetta is available at the deli counter of most major supermarkets, but if you can't find it, substitute thick-sliced bacon, cut into ¼-inch strips. Besides using it in this recipe, you can use pancetta in Lemony Pasta Carbonara with Sugar Snap Peas (page 31) and in almost any other dish that calls for bacon.

orzo with spring vegetables and lavender

If you like risotto, but you don't like the stirring and stirring, this orzo is for you. It has similar flavors, although admittedly, not risotto's intense creaminess. (If you don't mind the stirring and stirring, try Steak, Porcini, and Parmesan Risotto, page 180.)

Try serving the dish as a pasta first course. • SERVES 4

8 ounces orzo (about 1⅛ cup)
1 cup reduced-sodium chicken or vegetable broth
1 carrot, cut into ¼-inch dice
¼ cup fresh or frozen peas, thawed if frozen
1½ teaspoons chopped fresh thyme
4 scallions, white and light green parts only, thinly sliced
½ cup grated Parmesan cheese (2½ to 3 ounces)
½ teaspoon dried lavender flowers (see below)
¼ teaspoon coarse kosher salt, plus more to taste
⅛ teaspoon freshly ground black pepper, plus more to taste
3 tablespoons extra virgin olive oil, divided
¼ cup Viognier, or other dry white wine
Fresh lavender sprigs or fresh chives for garnish, optional

▦ In a medium pot of boiling well-salted water (1 tablespoon of coarse kosher salt per quart), cook the orzo until barely al dente, 6 to 8 minutes. Drain and return the orzo to the pot, along with the broth, carrot, peas, if fresh, and thyme. Bring to a boil over medium-high heat, reduce to a simmer, and cook, stirring constantly, until the broth is absorbed, the orzo is al dente, and the carrots are tender, about 5 minutes. (If the liquid evaporates before the ingredients are cooked, add water a few tablespoonfuls at a time.)

▦ Remove the pot from the heat and add the peas, if previously frozen, scallions, cheese, lavender flowers, salt, pepper, and 1 tablespoon of the olive oil, stirring until the peas are heated through and the cheese is melted. Stir in the wine.

▦ Transfer the orzo to individual bowls, drizzle with the remaining 2 tablespoons of olive oil, garnish with the lavender sprigs or chives, if using, and serve.

NOTE Dried lavender flowers are available at specialty food stores and in the bulk dried herbs and flowers section at many natural food stores. Besides using them in this recipe, you can use them in a dried herb blend called herbes de Provence, which is featured in Herbes de Provence Salmon Skewers with Provençal Aïoli (page 125), and you can sprinkle them into baked goods or over roasting poultry.

riesling

Ah, Riesling. One of my favorite wines. It's fruity, it's refreshing, it's light, and it's great for both sipping and for pairing with food.

If it's new to you, you're not alone. Riesling (REES-ling) has, for centuries, been considered one of the world's truly great grapes—but we're just now getting the message here in the States. That message, though, is coming on strong. Some say that Riesling is the fastest-growing white wine in the country.

If it's not new to you, you might have had Riesling in the past and think of it as a sweet wine. While it's true that Riesling is made in many styles, from very dry to very sweet—and everything in between—with Riesling's growth in popularity, more and more of the drier styles are showing up on shelves. And they're well worth trying.

riesling by another name

• *White Riesling, Johannisberg Riesling.* There are a lot of wines and grape names with the word *Riesling* in them—but these two, along with Riesling Renano, are the only ones made from the true Riesling grape. Johannisberg Riesling was once a popular name for California Rieslings, but it's not used anymore.

pairing with riesling

Although there are, of course, nuances to Riesling, the most important factors in food and wine pairing aren't a wine's nuances, but its broad strokes. If you learn a wine's overall characteristics and combine that information with the General Pairing Tips (page 6), you'll have a near-perfect pairing every time.

Broad characteristics:
• dry to off-dry (very slightly sweet)
• medium to high in acidity, crispness, or brightness
• little or no tannins
• light to medium weight
• light to medium intensity

Pairs well with dishes that are:
• not sweet to very slightly sweet
• medium to high in acidity, crispness, or brightness

- light to medium weight
- light to medium intensity

(Because the wine has little or no tannins, they're not a factor.)

For example, honey-baked ham, fish with salsa verde, or sweet-and-sour chicken.

fine-tuning

A touch of sweetness in the wine means you can afford only a touch of sweetness in the food. In other words, don't go crazy adding fruits or other sugary ingredients like candied nuts to your Riesling pairings. If you can't help yourself and the sweetness in the food starts making the wine taste sour, add acid to the food—especially acids that are light and fruity like the wine, such as lemon or lime juice, white or golden balsamic vinegar, or rice vinegar.

In addition to tasting great with food that's a little sweet, an off-dry Riesling can also work with food that's a little spicy.

other nuances

Once you have a pairing that's working on the basis of sweetness, acidity, weight, and intensity, you can start playing with subtler nuances.

Some of the subtle flavors that you might find in a Riesling include stone fruits, apple, pear, tropical fruits, citrus, honey, floral notes, smoke, and steely and even petrol-like notes. So it works to add those flavors, or foods that complement them, to your dishes.

other thoughts

Some foods that are considered classic pairings with Riesling are Asian food (especially Thai food), pork and ham, poultry (even gamier types like goose and duck), fish and shellfish, smoked fish, and moderately spicy dishes.

tropical fruit salsa and chips

Here's a deliciously fruity salsa that's sweet but not overly so—thanks to plenty of lime juice and the overall mellowing influence of avocado. It's that slight sweetness that helps the dish pair with Riesling, which can have a touch of sugar.

Sometimes, though, you'll see Riesling labeled "dry Riesling," which means it's lacking that sugar. While most of the recipes in this chapter will go with either style, this isn't one of them, so steer clear of a dry Riesling here.

If you have leftover salsa, serve it with chicken, fish, or pork. The resulting dish will—you guessed it—pair well with Riesling.

• **SERVES 8 TO 12**

1 mango, peeled, pitted, and cut into ¼-inch dice
1 papaya, peeled, seeded, and cut into ¼-inch dice
1 avocado, peeled, pitted, and cut into ¼-inch dice
1 jalapeño, cored, seeded, and finely diced
¼ red onion, finely diced
¼ cup coarsely chopped fresh cilantro
¼ cup fresh lime juice (from 3 or 4 limes), or more to taste
½ teaspoon coarse kosher salt, or more to taste
Tortilla chips, for serving

▓ In a medium bowl, combine the mango, papaya, avocado, jalapeño, onion, cilantro, lime juice, and salt. Taste, ideally with your wine, and add more lime juice and/or salt if you like. Serve with the chips on the side.

FOOD & WINE TIP If your fruit is particularly sweet, you might notice that the salsa makes your wine seem a little sour. To fix this, just add more lime juice, a teaspoon or two at a time, until the salsa and the wine nicely complement each other.

edamame wontons with gingered soy sauce

These bright, flavorful wontons are a great combination of light and refreshing on the inside yet crisp and chewy on the outside. The dipping sauce adds both zing and savory notes.

Serve them at a finger-foods party, as a first course for an Asian-themed dinner, or alongside your favorite stir-fry. • **SERVES 6**

2 cups shelled edamame (green soybeans), thawed if frozen, divided
¼ cup fresh lemon juice (from about 2 lemons)
¼ cup loosely packed fresh cilantro leaves
6 tablespoons aji-mirin sweet cooking rice seasoning (Japanese cooking wine), divided (see below)
2 scallions, white and light green parts only, thinly sliced, divided
36 round wonton wrappers (see below)
⅔ cup soy sauce
1½ teaspoons freshly grated ginger
1 teaspoon sesame oil
About ½ cup safflower, sunflower, peanut, or other high-heat cooking oil

▓ Set ½ cup of the edamame aside. In the bowl of a food processor, combine the remaining edamame with the lemon juice, cilantro, and ¼ cup of the aji-mirin and process to form a coarse paste, scraping down the bowl as necessary. Transfer the mixture to a medium bowl. Stir in the reserved edamame and all but 1 teaspoon of the scallions. Set the remaining scallions aside. (If you're making the wontons more than a day in advance, add all of the scallions to the edamame mixture.)

▓ Arrange 6 wonton wrappers on a work surface (keep the remaining wrappers covered with a damp kitchen towel). Spoon about 2 teaspoons of the edamame mixture onto each of the 6 wrappers, moisten the edges with water, fold the wrapper over the filling, and press to seal. Place the filled wontons in a single layer on a baking sheet. Repeat with the remaining wonton wrappers. (You can prepare the wontons in advance, storing them covered in the refrigerator for up to a day or in the freezer for several months. Thaw in the refrigerator before proceeding.)

▓ In a small bowl, combine the soy sauce, ginger, sesame oil, and the remaining 2 tablespoons of aji-mirin. Set aside. (You can prepare the soy sauce mixture up to a day in advance, storing it covered in the refrigerator.)

(continued on next page)

In a large nonstick skillet over medium heat, warm 3 tablespoons of the safflower oil. Working in batches and without crowding the skillet, add the wontons and cook until browned, about 1½ minutes per side. Transfer to a paper towel–lined plate. Repeat with the remaining wontons, adding more oil as necessary.

(You can also boil the wontons. Bring a large pot of well-salted water [1 tablespoon of coarse kosher salt per quart] to a boil. Add 1 tablespoon of canola, grapeseed, or other neutral-flavored oil. Add 8 to 10 wontons and cook until they float to the surface, about 2 minutes. Use a slotted spoon to transfer the cooked wontons to a platter or to individual plates. Repeat with the remaining wontons.)

Transfer the soy sauce mixture to a small serving bowl or to individual small bowls. Top with the reserved scallions, if you have them. Serve the wontons warm with the soy sauce mixture on the side.

NOTES Aji-mirin is available in the ethnic or Asian section of most major supermarkets. Besides using it in this recipe, you can also use it in Lettuce Cup Pork (page 81) and in other stir-fry sauces.

Wonton wrappers are available in the refrigerated part of the dairy or produce section at most major supermarkets. Besides using them in this recipe, you can use them to make other filled foods and they can be cut into strips, fried, and added to salads, as in a Chinese chicken salad.

FOOD & WINE TIP It's not a coincidence that a lot of the recipes in this chapter are Asian-inspired—Asian food has a natural affinity to Riesling.

pear, apple sausage, and swiss cheese bites

You hardly need a recipe to know how to put cubes of cheese, slices of sausage, and pieces of pear on a toothpick. But if I didn't include one, you wouldn't know how well the combination goes with Riesling.

As for the accompanying honey-mustard sauce, I used to use it on ham and Brie sandwiches at the café I owned. Customers would eat the sandwich and then beg me for the sauce recipe. I'd tell them, "Just mix honey and mustard." And every time, it took convincing for them to believe there was nothing more to it than that.

It just goes to show that sometimes the simplest combinations can be the most amazing! • **SERVES 6**

6 tablespoons Dijon mustard
2 tablespoons honey
12 ounces precooked apple sausages, cut into ½-inch slices
(you should have 40 to 50 pieces)
12 ounces Swiss cheese, cut into ¾-inch dice (you should
have 40 to 50 pieces)
1 firm-ripe pear, cored and cut into ¾-inch dice (you should
have 40 to 50 pieces)

▦ In a small bowl, whisk together the mustard and honey. Set aside. (You can prepare the mustard mixture up to 3 days in advance, storing it covered in the refrigerator.)

▦ Heat a large skillet over medium-high heat. Add the sausages and cook, stirring occasionally, until nicely browned and heated through, 3 to 4 minutes. Transfer the sausages to a plate and set aside to cool slightly.

▦ Meanwhile, drizzle the mustard mixture decoratively onto a platter or onto individual plates, dividing it evenly.

▦ When the sausage is cool enough to handle, skewer a piece of cheese, a piece of sausage, and a piece of pear onto a toothpick. Repeat with the remaining cheese, sausages, and pear, arranging the toothpicks on top of the mustard. Serve warm.

spicy shrimp sushi rolls

Of course, sake is great with sushi. I also enjoy a good martini with it. But Riesling and sushi is probably my favorite combination of all. The wine accentuates both the sweet and savory nature of sushi, and the hint of sweetness that comes with most Rieslings deliciously counters the spice from wasabi, chili sauce, or both.

Don't be daunted by the idea of making sushi at home. It's really quite easy once you get the hang of it. And even if your first few rolls don't turn out perfectly, they'll still taste great. • **MAKES 4 ROLLS, TO SERVE 4 TO 6**

¼ cup mayonnaise
1½ teaspoons chili sauce, such as Sriracha, or more to taste (see note on page 41)
4 approximately 7½ x 8½-inch sheets nori (see below)
About 3 cups prepared Sushi Rice (recipe follows)
4 ounces cooked shrimp, coarsely chopped
½ small cucumber, peeled, halved lengthwise, seeded, and cut lengthwise into long, thin slices
½ small carrot, julienned
Soy sauce, for serving
Wasabi paste, for serving (see below)
Pickled ginger, for serving (see below)
Special equipment: bamboo sushi mat (see below)

▒ In a small bowl, combine the mayonnaise and chili sauce. Taste and add more chili sauce if you like. Set aside. (You can prepare the mayonnaise mixture up to 3 days in advance, storing it covered in the refrigerator.)

▒ Place a bamboo sushi mat on a work surface, with the sticks in the mat parallel to you. Place a sheet of nori on the mat, shiny side (if there is one) down, shorter edge toward you. Have a small shallow bowl of water nearby.

▒ Dampen your hands in the water, shaking off the excess. Use your fingers to press about ¾ cup of sushi rice onto the nori, covering ¾ of the length of the sheet and the entire width, leaving 2 or 3 inches from the farthest edge uncovered. (If the rice sticks to your hands as you work, redampen them in the water). Drizzle about 1 tablespoon of the mayonnaise mixture on top of the rice in a line parallel to you, about 1 inch in from the closest edge. Top with ¼ of the shrimp, ¼ of the cucumber, and ¼ of the carrot.

▦ Holding the fillings firmly in place with the fingertips of both hands, use your thumbs to lift the edge of the mat closest to you up and over, enclosing the fillings. Squeeze gently to make a compact roll. Raise the end of the mat slightly to avoid rolling it in with the nori, and continue rolling, squeezing occasionally, until the sushi is completely rolled in a tight cylinder. If necessary, dampen the edge of the nori to help seal it, then set the roll aside for a minute or two. Using a sharp knife, slice the roll into 8 pieces. Repeat with the remaining ingredients, making 4 rolls total.

▦ Serve the sushi with the soy sauce, wasabi, and pickled ginger on the side.

sushi rice · *Makes about 3 cups*

1 cup short-grain white rice or sushi rice
3 tablespoons seasoned rice vinegar

Place the rice in a strainer and rinse it under cold water until the water runs clear. Transfer the rice to a 1-quart saucepan. Add 1¼ cups of cold water and bring to a boil over high heat. Reduce the heat to low, cover, and cook until the water is absorbed and the rice is tender, about 15 minutes. Remove from the heat and let stand, covered, for 15 minutes.

Turn the cooked rice out into a large, shallow bowl or dish. Use a rice paddle or spatula and a slashing motion to spread the rice evenly in the bowl (don't toss or the rice can become gummy). Drizzle the vinegar over the rice. With the same slashing motion, mix until the grains are coated and glossy. Cover with a damp kitchen towel and set aside to cool. (You can prepare sushi rice up to several hours in advance, keeping it covered with a damp towel at room temperature.)

NOTES Nori (seaweed sheets), wasabi paste, and pickled ginger are available in the ethnic or Asian section of most major supermarkets. Besides using them in this recipe, you can use them in other Asian or Asian-themed dishes.

Bamboo sushi mats are available in the ethnic or Asian section or in the utensils section of most major supermarkets. They're also available at cookware stores. Cover the sushi mat with plastic wrap to make it easy to clean.

pan-toasted pâté with pistachios

One of the all-time great, classic food and wine pairings is foie gras and Sauternes, a sweet wine from the Bordeaux region of France. It's a sublimely rich, sweet, salty, decadent combination if there ever was one. If you're a foie gras fan, definitely make it your business to try it some time.

Meanwhile, try this combination of pistachio-encrusted pâté and refreshing Riesling, which ain't too shabby either. And while it's traditional to serve pâté with cornichons (tiny, sweet pickles) and Dijon mustard, here we're using sweet-hot mustard because it's a much better match for the wine. • **SERVES 4**

One ¾-inch-thick slice liver pâté (about ½ pound)
⅔ cup chopped raw pistachios
8 slices challah, egg bread, or buttermilk bread, crusts removed,
   quartered diagonally, and toasted (see page 13)
¼ cup sweet-hot mustard

▧ Cut the pâté in half widthwise. Cut each half diagonally, into triangles. Cut each triangle in half horizontally, halving its thickness. You should have eight ⅜-inch-thick triangles.

▧ Place the pistachios on a plate. Gently press the pâté into the nuts, covering both sides. Place the coated pâté on a plate and freeze for at least an hour. (You can freeze the pâté, covered, for up to a week.)

▧ Heat a large nonstick skillet over medium heat. Add the pâté triangles and cook until browned, about 1½ minutes. Carefully turn the triangles and brown the other side, about 1½ minutes. Arrange the pâté, toasts, and mustard on a platter or on individual plates, dividing them evenly, and serve.

jalapeño lime ceviche

Right now in San Francisco, about an hour from where I live in Napa, ceviche is totally hot. It seems like there's a new Peruvian restaurant opening every week, with a dozen ceviches on the menu. Some say it's the new sushi. Which would be fine with me—like sushi, ceviche combines bright flavors, crunchy and smooth textures, and a refreshingly cool temperature. I love it.

And ceviche is a snap to make. Just mix your ingredients and set the ceviche aside, stirring occasionally. The fish essentially cooks in the acid of the lime juice.

Use the freshest, best-quality seafood you can find, ideally from a good fishmonger. Tell him or her you're making ceviche and use whatever white-fleshed fish he or she recommends. • SERVES 6

About 7 limes
1 pound skinless white-fleshed fish fillets, such as halibut,
    tilapia, sturgeon, or a combination, cut into ½-inch dice
½ red bell pepper, cored, seeded, and cut into ¼-inch dice
¼ small red onion, finely diced
2 jalapeños, cored, seeded, and finely diced
½ teaspoon coarse kosher salt, or more to taste
3 tablespoons chopped fresh cilantro
About 30 tortilla chips, for serving

▒ Zest 4 of the limes. Juice the zested limes plus enough of the remaining limes to yield ½ cup of juice. In a large nonreactive bowl, combine the zest, juice, fish, red pepper, onion, jalapeños, and salt. Set aside in the refrigerator, stirring occasionally, until the fish becomes opaque, about 1 hour.

▒ Stir in the cilantro. Taste, ideally with your wine, and add more lime juice and/or salt if you like. Spoon the ceviche into decorative glasses and garnish each serving with a tortilla chip. Serve with the remaining chips on the side.

FOOD & WINE TIP When it comes to pairing wines with spicy foods, generally, there are two ways to go: You can choose wines with really ripe, fruity, and even lightly sweet flavors, or you can go with wines with oakiness. For something light, like this dish, opt for the former. For heavier foods, go with the latter—for example, Zinfandel and barbecue.

watercress salad with apricots and almond-crusted brie

You won't believe how incredible these little wedges of toasted, melty, almond-crusted Brie taste. They would be great to serve on their own, with Chardonnay or Viognier. Adding the dressing, the slightly spicy watercress, and the slightly sweet apricots, though, makes the dish a natural for Riesling.

Using dried apricots, which tend to be less sweet than fresh ones, keeps the dish from being too sweet and making the wine taste sour. • **SERVES 4**

½ cup sliced raw almonds
One 8-ounce round Brie cheese, cut into 12 wedges
¼ cup white or golden balsamic vinegar (see note on page 29)
1 shallot, minced
1 teaspoon coarse kosher salt
¼ teaspoon freshly ground black pepper
3 tablespoons almond oil (see below)
3 tablespoons canola, grapeseed, or other neutral-flavored oil
6 cups loosely packed watercress leaves (about 4 ounces)
½ cup chopped dried apricots

▨ Place the almonds on a plate. Gently press the cut sides of the cheese wedges into the nuts. Place the coated wedges on a plate and freeze for at least an hour. (You can freeze the cheese, covered, for up to a week.)

▨ In a small bowl, combine the vinegar, shallot, salt, and pepper, whisking to dissolve the salt. Whisk in the oils. (You can prepare the dressing up to 3 days in advance, storing it covered in the refrigerator. Return to room temperature before proceeding.)

▨ In a large bowl, combine the watercress, apricots, and dressing to taste. Arrange the salad on a platter or on individual plates, dividing it evenly.

▨ Heat a large nonstick skillet over medium heat. Add the Brie wedges, crusted side down, and cook until browned, about 1½ minutes. Carefully turn the wedges and brown the other crusted side, about 1½ minutes. Arrange the Brie wedges around the salad and serve.

> **NOTE** Almond oil is available at better supermarkets and specialty food stores, but if you can't find it, substitute another nut oil or a neutral-flavored oil. Besides using it in this recipe, you can use almond oil in other salads, pastas, muffins, and cookies.

chicken satay with peanut sauce

Here's a restaurant-quality dish that's super-easy to make at home.

If by some miracle you have leftovers, shred the chicken and toss it with the peanut sauce and just-cooked fettuccini noodles. Toss in some thinly sliced celery, scallions, and cilantro, and you'll have a yummy Asian noodle salad—which would, of course, be perfect with Riesling. • SERVES 6

⅓ cup natural peanut butter
1 tablespoon seasoned rice vinegar
1 tablespoon sesame oil
1 teaspoon freshly grated ginger
1 clove garlic, pressed through a garlic press or minced
⅛ teaspoon coarse kosher salt
⅛ teaspoon dried crushed red pepper flakes
1 cup Riesling, or other dry or off-dry white wine, divided
9 tablespoon soy sauce, divided
2 tablespoons packed light brown sugar
1½ pounds chicken tenders, or boneless, skinless chicken breasts cut into ½-inch strips (you should have about 18 tenders or strips)
6 sprigs fresh cilantro
Special equipment: about eighteen 8-inch skewers, soaked in water for at least 10 minutes if they're wood or bamboo

▓ In a small saucepan over medium heat, combine the peanut butter, vinegar, sesame oil, ginger, garlic, salt, red pepper, ½ cup of the wine, and 1 tablespoon of the soy sauce. Bring to a gentle boil, stirring until the mixture thickens. Remove from the heat and set aside to cool to room temperature.

▓ In a medium bowl, combine the brown sugar with the remaining ½ cup of wine and the remaining ½ cup of soy sauce, whisking to dissolve the sugar. (You can prepare the peanut sauce and the wine mixture up to 2 days in advance, storing both covered in the refrigerator.)

▓ Place the chicken in a large resealable bag, add the wine mixture, and seal, squeezing out as much air as possible. Set aside in the refrigerator for 1 to 3 hours, turning occasionally.

▓ Prepare the grill to medium heat and lightly oil the grate. Remove the chicken from the marinade and thread it onto skewers, one strip per skewer. Grill the chicken until it's cooked through, 2½ to 3 minutes per side.

▓ Arrange the skewers on a platter or on individual plates with the peanut sauce on the side. Garnish with the cilantro and serve.

lettuce cup pork

Lettuce cups are Asian-influenced, sometimes spicy, ground meat mixtures you eat taco-style, with a lettuce leaf in place of the tortilla. At Betelnut, one of my favorite restaurants in San Francisco, my husband and I have been known to laze away the whole afternoon sitting at a sidewalk table, eating lettuce cups, and drinking Riesling. • SERVES 6

¼ cup soy sauce
3 tablespoons aji-mirin sweet cooking rice seasoning (Japanese cooking wine) (see note on page 72)
3 tablespoons oyster sauce (see below)
1 tablespoon cornstarch
12 large iceberg lettuce leaves
1 tablespoon safflower, sunflower, peanut, or other high-heat cooking oil
1 pound ground pork
1 red bell pepper, cored, seeded, and finely diced
4 ounces shiitake mushrooms, stems removed, finely diced (you should have about 2 cups)
6 scallions, white and light green parts only, thinly sliced
One 8-ounce can water chestnuts, drained and finely diced
½ cup pine nuts, toasted (see page 26)
¼ cup chopped fresh basil

▓ In a small bowl, whisk together the soy sauce, aji-mirin, oyster sauce, and cornstarch. Set aside.

▓ Using kitchen shears, round the edges of the lettuce leaves so that each one makes a small bowl. Set aside. (You can prepare the soy sauce mixture and the lettuce leaves up to a day in advance, storing them covered in the refrigerator.)

▓ In a wok or large skillet over medium-high heat, warm the oil until shimmering. Add the pork and stir-fry until no longer pink, about 3 minutes. Add the red pepper and stir-fry for 1 minute. Add the mushrooms and stir-fry for 2 minutes. Add the scallions, water chestnuts, and pine nuts and stir-fry for 1 minute. Add the soy sauce mixture and stir until the sauce thickens. Remove from the heat and stir in the basil.

▓ Serve hot or at room temperature with the lettuce leaves on the side, scooping the meat mixture onto the lettuce leaf "cups" and eating them like a taco.

NOTE Oyster sauce is available in the ethnic or Asian section of most major supermarkets. Besides using it in this recipe, you can use it in other Asian dishes and stir-fries.

tea-smoked sturgeon

One of the first times that the food and wine pairing lightbulb
went off in my head, when I had a combination that really under-
scored how good a good combination can be, was over dinner at a
then-new, beautiful French-Vietnamese restaurant in San Francisco
called Le Colonial. It was one of those perfect evenings—the atmo-
sphere, the service, the food, the company—but the best part was
the smoked Chilean sea bass with a glass of Riesling.

These days, sadly, Chilean sea bass is off my plate. According
to Seafood Watch, a program from the Monterey Bay Aquarium
(montereybayaquarium.org) designed to raise awareness about
seafood sustainability, most Chilean sea bass isn't a good choice because of illegal and ecologically harmful fishing practices. Luckily,
sturgeon is just as good for channeling that fantastic fish and wine
combination—if not better. (Seafood Watch recommends avoiding
imported sturgeon.) Or ask your fishmonger what he or she recommends—whatever is in season will likely be the best tasting and
least expensive. • SERVES 4 TO 6

⅔ cup coarse kosher salt
⅓ cup packed light brown sugar
¼ cup fresh lemon juice (from about 2 lemons)
1 teaspoon Chinese five-spice powder (see note on page 60)
1 pound skinless sturgeon fillets, ¾- to 1-inch thick
2 tea bags (not herbal)
⅔ cup shredded carrot
⅓ cup shredded daikon radish
1 lemon, cut into wedges
Special equipment: stovetop smoker (see below)

▦ In a large bowl, combine 5½ cups of cool water with the salt,
brown sugar, lemon juice, and five-spice powder, whisking to dissolve the salt and sugar. Place the fish in a shallow dish, pan, or other
container and pour in enough of the saltwater mixture to cover (discard
any remaining mixture or save it for another use). Place a light cup or
small plate on top of the fish to keep it submerged, cover the entire
setup with plastic wrap, and refrigerate for 45 minutes.

▦ Remove the fish from the brine and, if you like, cut it into 4 to 6
pieces. Place the fish on a lightly oiled wire rack (the rack from the
smoker is fine). Place the rack on a rimmed baking sheet and set it
aside in a cool, ideally breezy, place for 1 hour. (You can create a

breeze by placing an electric fan on low speed nearby.) This will form a thin glaze on the fish called the pellicle, which gives the fish better color, flavor, and texture.

▓ Cut open the tea bags and empty the leaves into the bottom of the smoker. Place the drip catcher on top of the leaves, the wire rack on top of the drip catcher, and the fish on the wire rack. Cover the smoker, leaving the lid very slightly ajar, and place it on the stovetop over medium heat. As soon as you see any wisps of smoke escaping, close the lid tightly and smoke for 12 minutes, until the fish is cooked through.

▓ Arrange the carrot, radish, and lemon wedges on a platter or on individual plates, top with the fish, and serve.

is it dry or sweet?

Often it's hard to tell from the outside of the bottle what the wine inside is going to taste like. But it's especially confounding with both Riesling and Gewürztraminer, which can come in a range of sweetness levels, from bone-dry to sticky-sweet.

Sometimes there will be hints. The label might say "dry" or "trocken," which is *dry* in German. It might say "Kabinett" or "Spätlese," which are German terms for off-dry, or very slightly sweet, wines. Or it might say "Auslese," "Beerenauslese," "Eiswein," or "Trockenbeerenauslese," which are German terms for sweet or dessert wines. But often, it won't say anything.

The International Riesling Foundation is combating this confusion by promoting the use of a graphic to indicate the wine's sweetness (or lack thereof), like you might see on a jar of salsa indicating how hot it is. Meanwhile, if there's a description of the wine on the label, that can help. And—nothing takes the place of a knowledgeable retailer.

NOTE If you don't have a stovetop smoker, here's how to create a homemade version: Make 4 tight, 1-inch balls of foil and place them in the corners of a large roasting pan with a tight-fitting lid. Set a baking sheet or heatproof plate or platter inside the pan, resting on the foil balls, to act as a drip catcher. Set a wire rack on top of that. Make sure the lid still fits tightly over the whole thing.

FOOD & WINE TIP This recipe also pairs well with Sauvignon Blanc, especially the type known as Fumé Blanc. Fumé Blanc often has some oak aging, which helps it pair with smoky dishes like this one.

gewürz-
traminer

think of Gewürztraminer as a full-bodied Riesling. Now, that statement may cause some Gewürz-aphiles to shudder, because there are, of course, differences. But both are fruity, bright, fragrant, often floral, and always drinkable. Both are great food wines. And both are German.

Both, too, are somewhat underappreciated in the United States. In the case of Gewürztraminer, it could be simply because the name is hard to pronounce (gah-VERTZ-trah-mee-ner). But it could also be that, like Riesling, Gewürztraminer has a stigma of being a sweet wine, when in fact, like Riesling, it comes in all styles.

While Riesling is typically low in alcohol and light, however, Gewürz is typically lush and full-bodied, often with riper fruit flavors. Perhaps the most distinctive thing about Gewürztraminer, though, is the sometimes spicy quality. (*Gewürz* is German for "spice.") But not spicy like a hot chile. Spicy like cinnamon, anise, allspice, and nutmeg. Baking spices. Warming spices. "Mmmm" spices . . .

gewürztraminer by another name

Thankfully, with a name that's already a mouthful, there are no others that this varietal commonly goes by.

pairing with gewürztraminer

Although there are, of course, nuances to Gewürztraminer, the most important factors in food and wine pairing aren't a wine's nuances, but its broad strokes. If you learn a wine's overall characteristics and combine that information with the General Pairing Tips (page 6), you'll have a near-perfect pairing every time.

Broad characteristics:
- dry to off-dry (very slightly sweet)
- medium in acidity, crispness, or brightness
- little or no tannins
- medium to heavy weight
- medium to strong intensity

Pairs well with dishes that are:
- not sweet to very slightly sweet
- medium in acidity, crispness, or brightness

- medium to heavy weight
- medium to strong intensity

(Because the wine has little or no tannins, they're not a factor.)

For example, blue cheese and walnut bread, turkey with apple stuffing, or butternut squash soup.

fine-tuning

Here, the same caution as with Riesling: a touch of sweetness in the wine means you can afford only a touch of sweetness in the food. So don't go crazy adding sugary ingredients to your Gewürztraminer pairings. If you end up with too much sweetness and the wine is tasting sour, try adding acidic ingredients—but use richer ones like buttermilk, yogurt, or sour cream since the wine itself is also rich.

In addition to tasting great with food that's a little sweet, an off-dry Gewürztraminer can also work with food that's a little spicy.

other nuances

Once you have a pairing that's working on the basis of sweetness, acidity, weight, and intensity, you can start playing with subtler nuances.

Some of the subtle flavors that you might find in a Gewürztraminer include stone fruits, apple, pear, tropical fruits, honey, floral notes, and baking spices. So it works to add those flavors, or foods that complement them, to your dishes.

other thoughts

Some foods that are considered classic pairings with Gewürztraminer are Asian foods (especially richer and moderately spicy dishes like curries); pungent, strong, and even stinky cheeses; sausages and smoked meats; pork and ham; turkey, duck, goose, and other gamier poultry; and rich egg dishes like quiche.

cinnamon and cream cheese tea sandwiches

These little snack sandwiches are sophisticated, yet easy to put together with readily available ingredients. They'd be ideal as accompaniments to a late-afternoon glass of wine with friends or as part of a wine-tasting party.

Sour cream, lemon juice, and salt mixed into the cream cheese, plus tannin-y toasted pecans garnishing the edges, make the sandwiches more suited to grown-up tastes—and, of course, the wine.

• SERVES 4

One 3-ounce package cream cheese, room temperature
2 tablespoons sour cream
1 teaspoon fresh lemon juice
½ teaspoon coarse kosher salt
¼ teaspoon ground cinnamon
12 slices cinnamon raisin bread
⅓ cup chopped pecans, toasted (see page 26)

▦ In a small bowl, combine the cream cheese, sour cream, lemon juice, salt, and cinnamon. (You can prepare the cream cheese mixture up to a day in advance, storing it covered in the refrigerator.)

▦ Set 2 tablespoons of the cream cheese mixture aside. Spread the remaining cream cheese mixture evenly on 6 slices of the bread. Top with the 6 remaining slices of bread. Trim the crusts and cut the sandwiches in half.

▦ Place the pecans on a plate. Spread the reserved cream cheese mixture along one edge of each of the tea sandwiches and gently press that edge into the nuts. (You can prepare the sandwiches up to 4 hours in advance, storing them covered in the refrigerator.)

▦ Serve the sandwiches cold or at room temperature.

red hawk cheese with star anise syrup

This is a very simple recipe, but one with beautifully distinct flavors.

Red Hawk is a creamy, slightly pungent, and absolutely to-die-for cheese from Cowgirl Creamery. You can buy it at better cheese shops or at www.cowgirlcreamery.com. In a pinch, substitute Port-Salut, which you can find in most major supermarkets.

The star anise add slightly Christmas-y spice, but also an exotic, haunting warmth. Besides using it in this recipe, you can use star anise in soups, stews, braised dishes, and even desserts. Look for it at a better supermarket or specialty food store, or order it from Penzeys Spices or Amazon.com. It's worth finding. • SERVES 6 TO 8

¼ cup Gewürztraminer, or other dry or off-dry white wine
¼ cup honey
3 whole star anise (see above)
1½ teaspoons cornstarch dissolved in 1 tablespoon cold water
One 12-ounce round Red Hawk cheese (see above)
One 4¼-ounce package table water crackers, for serving

▓ In a small saucepan over medium heat, combine the wine, honey, and star anise and bring to a boil. Remove the saucepan from the heat, cover, and set aside to steep for 15 minutes.

▓ Stir in the cornstarch mixture and return the saucepan to medium heat. Cook, stirring, until the mixture comes to a boil and thickens, 60 to 90 seconds. Strain out the star anise (reserve it for a garnish), and set the syrup aside to cool to room temperature. (You can prepare the star anise syrup up to 3 days in advance, storing it and the reserved star anise covered in the refrigerator. Return the syrup to room temperature before serving.)

▓ Place the cheese on a platter or large plate and allow it to come to room temperature. Drizzle the star anise syrup over and around the cheese and garnish with the reserved star anise. Serve with the crackers on the side.

FOOD & WINE TIP It's classic to pair a pungent cheese like Red Hawk with a sweet or dessert wine. If you go that route, because the sweeter wine can stand up to a sweeter syrup, increase the honey in the recipe to ½ cup, decrease the wine to 2 tablespoons, and omit the cornstarch mixture. Killer.

chicken, nectarine, and macadamia nut salad

This salad is one of my favorite summer flavor combinations. It's especially good, and easy to prepare, using breasts from store-bought rotisserie chicken. • **SERVES 6**

3 tablespoons seasoned rice vinegar
2 tablespoons packed light brown sugar
½ teaspoon coarse kosher salt
¼ teaspoon freshly grated ginger
¼ teaspoon freshly ground black pepper
4 teaspoons canola, grapeseed, or other neutral-flavored oil
2 teaspoons sesame oil
10 cups loosely packed mixed salad greens (about 5 ounces)
1 freestone (the flesh doesn't cling to the pit) yellow nectarine, pitted and thinly sliced
½ small red onion, halved and thinly sliced
½ cup coarsely chopped fresh cilantro
2 small cooked chicken breasts (10 to 12 ounces)
¼ cup chopped macadamia nuts, toasted (see page 26)

▓ In a small bowl, combine the vinegar, brown sugar, salt, ginger, and pepper, whisking to dissolve the salt and sugar. Whisk in the oils. Set aside. (You can prepare the dressing up to 3 days in advance, storing it covered in the refrigerator.)

▓ In a large mixing bowl, combine the greens, nectarine, onion, and cilantro. Add a light amount of dressing and toss. Arrange the salad on a platter or on individual plates, dividing it evenly.

▓ Cut the chicken breasts on a diagonal into ½-inch slices. Arrange the chicken on top of the salad. Drizzle some of the remaining dressing over the chicken, top with the macadamia nuts, and serve.

FOOD & WINE TIP If your nectarines are particularly sweet, this salad will be best with an off-dry, or slightly sweet, Gewürztraminer. If you don't know if your Gewürtz is dry or off-dry—the label might have some clues, but not always—don't worry about it.

curried onion rings with apricot dipping sauce

I know, I know. Frying. It's such a mess, such a hassle, and so fattening! But you don't do it every day, and some dishes are worth it. Like this one. These onion rings are so yummy and really not that much of a mess or hassle. Honest. • SERVES 6 TO 8

½ cup all-fruit apricot preserves
1½ teaspoons cornstarch dissolved in ¼ cup cold water
½ teaspoon freshly grated ginger
1¼ teaspoons coarse kosher salt, divided, plus more for sprinkling
1 large onion (1 pound), ideally a sweet type such as Maui, cut crosswise into ⅓-inch-thick slices
1½ cups buttermilk
2 cups all-purpose flour
1 teaspoon curry powder
About 6 cups canola, grapeseed, or other neutral-flavored oil

░ In a small saucepan over medium heat, combine the apricot preserves, cornstarch mixture, ginger, and ¼ teaspoon of the salt, stirring until the mixture comes to a boil and thickens, 2 to 3 minutes. Remove from the heat and set aside to cool to room temperature. (You can prepare the dipping sauce up to 3 days in advance, storing it covered in the refrigerator. Return to room temperature before serving.)

░ Separate the onion slices into rings. Place the buttermilk in a shallow bowl. In a second shallow bowl, combine the flour, curry powder, and the remaining 1 teaspoon of salt. Place two baking sheets nearby.

░ One at a time, dip the onion rings in the buttermilk, then the flour mixture, shaking off the excess. Place the coated rings on the baking sheets.

░ Pour enough oil into a large, heavy stockpot so that the oil is 1 inch deep. Place the stockpot over medium heat and warm the oil to 370°F. Prepare a paper towel-lined platter or baking sheet.

░ Add the onion rings, 6 to 8 at a time, to the hot oil and cook, turning occasionally, until golden, about 2 minutes, adjusting the heat as necessary to maintain the temperature. Use tongs or a slotted spoon to transfer the cooked rings to the prepared platter.

░ While they're hot, sprinkle the onion rings with additional salt. Serve immediately, with the apricot dipping sauce on the side.

cold peach and mango soup shooters

This soup is just charmingly fun. It's pretty, it's tasty, and it's easy to make. A gulp or two, served in a little glass, makes for a quick, refreshing treat.

For best results, make it in the summer when fresh peaches are in season. In a pinch, you can use frozen fruit, but make sure it's unsweetened.

Serve the shooters at a standing-and-eating sort of party or as an amuse-bouche between courses. You can also serve the soup as a first course, which would be a great way to kick off a summery dinner party. If that's your plan, double the recipe for six one-cup servings. • MAKES 12 SHOOTERS (¼ CUP EACH)

2 limes
1 ripe freestone (the flesh doesn't cling to the pit) yellow peach, pitted and cut into chunks
1 ripe mango, peeled, pitted, and cut into chunks
¾ cup buttermilk
½ cup orange juice
½ teaspoon coarse kosher salt, or more to taste
Pinch cayenne pepper
12 fresh cilantro leaves

▓ Zest the limes. Set the zest aside. Juice the limes to yield 3 tablespoons of juice. In a blender or food processor, combine the lime juice, peach, mango, buttermilk, orange juice, salt, and cayenne and process until very smooth, scraping down the jar or bowl as necessary (you may have to do this in batches). Transfer the soup to a container and chill for at least 2 hours. (You can prepare the soup up to 3 days in advance, storing it covered in the refrigerator.)

▓ Taste, ideally with your wine and add more lime juice and/or salt if you like. Serve the soup chilled, each serving garnished with a cilantro leaf and some of the lime zest.

FOOD & WINE TIP If your fruit is particularly sweet, you might notice that the soup makes your wine seem a little sour. To fix this, just add more lime juice, a teaspoon or two at a time, until the soup and the wine nicely complement each other.

gouda and chutney quesadillas

If you like things with a little kick, use hot mango chutney in this recipe. It makes the quesadillas only mildly spicy—the cheese and avocado temper the heat—and the warmth nicely complements the spicy notes in the wine. • SERVES 3 TO 4

1½ teaspoons unsalted butter, softened, optional
Two 9- or 10-inch white flour tortillas
5 tablespoons mango or hot mango chutney, divided
2 cups shredded Gouda cheese (about 6 ounces)
¼ avocado, peeled, pitted, and thinly sliced

▓ Spread the butter, if using, on one side of each tortilla, dividing it evenly. Lay the tortillas, buttered side down, on a work surface. Spread 1 tablespoon of the chutney on half of each tortilla, leaving a 1-inch border at the edge. Arrange the cheese and avocado on top, dividing them evenly. Fold the tortillas in half over the fillings.

▓ In a large nonstick skillet over medium heat, cook the quesadillas, covered, until golden brown, 3 to 4 minutes. Carefully turn and cook, uncovered, until golden brown and the cheese has melted, 2 to 3 minutes.

▓ Cut each quesadilla into 6 or 8 wedges and serve, with the remaining 3 tablespoons of chutney on the side.

an argument for off-dry

Somewhere along the way, it became very uncool to admit to liking wine with even a hint of sweetness. And in fact, if you ask average wine drinkers what kind of wine they prefer, they'll say dry. But if you give them two wines to taste and ask which they prefer, chances are they'll choose the one that's very slightly sweet—not a sweet or dessert wine, but one that has just a touch of sugar to balance out the acidity and/or tannins, or bitterness, in a wine. In short, an off-dry wine.

I have no idea why or how off-dry wines became uncool. They absolutely shouldn't be, because not only can an off-dry wine be more pleasant to drink, but it often goes better with food. Why? Because many savory dishes, like barbecued chicken or pork chops with applesauce, have a touch of sweetness. And, per General Pairing Tip 1 (page 6), a similar sweetness in the wine will help prevent the food from making the wine taste sour.

In fact, many of today's hippest cuisines—Thai, Latin, Indian, Moroccan—have elements of sweetness that make them ideal for off-dry wines.

ham, apple, and cheddar monte cristo sandwiches

If you crossed an upscale, artisan ham and cheese sandwich with French toast, you'd get this Monte Cristo. The grilled, egg-dipped coating makes it incredibly rich and indulgent, and a perfect foil for similarly rich and heady Gewürztraminer. • **SERVES 4**

Six ¾-inch-thick slices crusty artisan, French, or sourdough bread
    (cut on an angle, if necessary, to make sandwich-sized slices)
2 tablespoons Dijon mustard
5 ounces medium-sharp Cheddar cheese, thinly sliced
3 ounces thinly sliced smoked ham
½ crisp-sweet apple, such as Fuji, cored and thinly sliced
3 large eggs
¼ cup (½ stick) unsalted butter

▓ Place 3 of the bread slices on a work surface. Spread with the mustard, dividing it evenly. Top with the cheese, ham, apple, and remaining 3 slices of bread, dividing them evenly.

▓ Beat the eggs in a large shallow bowl.

▓ In a very large skillet over medium-low heat, melt the butter. Dip both sides of each sandwich into the eggs, then place the sandwiches in the skillet. (If you don't have a skillet large enough to hold all three sandwiches, use one large and one small and distribute the butter, and then the sandwiches, between them.) Cover and cook until golden, about 4 minutes. Carefully turn and cook, covered, until golden brown, about 3 minutes.

▓ Cut the sandwiches in quarters and serve hot.

FOOD & WINE TIP Without the egg coating—just the plain sandwich—this recipe would pair well with Riesling.

rosé

absolutely, positively love Rosé.

Why? It's light, refreshing, and pairs perfectly with a warm afternoon. And, because it's typically high in fruit and low in alcohol, Rosé is a great food wine.

It works with barbecue or anything off the grill. It works with mildly spicy or smoky foods, with many ethnic cuisines, and even with dishes with a little sweetness. It's the perfect all-around wine, especially for the simply prepared, Mediterranean-inspired foods that have increasingly become American cuisine.

Maybe you're one of those people who has shunned Rosé, deciding it's too soda pop-y. I encourage you to reconsider. Over the last few years, more and more producers are making drier styles of Rosé, wines of quality and finesse. Give them a try—and you, too, might decide you like to drink pink.

rosé by another name

• *Rosato, Rosado*. These are the Italian and Spanish names, respectively, for Rosé. • *Vin Gris*. Literally "gray wine," a French name for very pale Rosés. Vin Gris is often made from Pinot Noir grapes. • *Blush*. Originally, this was a name for very pale Rosés, à la Vin Gris, but it's come to simply be another generic term for Rosé. • *White Zinfandel, White Grenache, White Merlot, etc*. These are U.S. names for Rosés made from specific grapes—Zinfandel, Grenache, Merlot, etc.

pairing with rosé

Although there are, of course, nuances to Rosé, the most important factors in food and wine pairing aren't a wine's nuances, but its broad strokes. If you learn a wine's overall characteristics and combine that information with the General Pairing Tips (page 6), you'll have a near-perfect pairing every time.

Broad characteristics:
- dry to off-dry (very slightly sweet)
- medium in acidity, crispness, or brightness
- little or no tannins
- light to medium weight
- light to medium intensity

Pairs well with dishes that are:
- not sweet to very slightly sweet
- medium in acidity, crispness, or brightness
- light to medium weight
- light to medium intensity

(Because the wine has little or no tannins, they're not a factor.)
For example, shrimp salad, a turkey sandwich with cranberry sauce, or barbecued chicken.

fine-tuning

As with Riesling and Gewürztraminer, a touch of sweetness in the wine means you can afford only a touch of sweetness in the food. So don't add too many sugary elements to your Rosé pairings. If it happens that sweet elements in the food are making the wine taste sour, try adding acidic ingredients, but use ones that are light, bright, and fruity like the wine—for example, lemon and lime juice, apple cider vinegar, and red wine vinegar.

In addition to tasting great with food that's a little sweet, an off-dry Rosé can also work with food that's a little spicy.

And remember that you can complement the fruitiness of Rosé not only by judiciously adding fruit to your dishes, but also by adding fruity elements. For example, use citrus zest, fruit-infused vinegars and oils, or even dried fruits, which tend to be less sweet than their fresh counterparts.

other nuances

Once you have a pairing that's working on the basis of sweetness, acidity, weight, and intensity, you can start playing with subtler nuances.

Some of the subtle flavors that you might find in a Rosé include red berries (especially raspberries, strawberries, and cranberries), cherries, pomegranate, grapefruit, and floral notes. So it works to add those flavors, or foods that complement them, to your dishes.

other thoughts

Some foods that are considered classic pairings with Rosé are deli meats, picnic foods, poultry, pork, fish and shellfish (especially grilled), barbecue and barbecue sauce, salads, and Mediterranean food.

killer guacamole

This guacamole is based on one my mom used to make. You'll see recipes with chopped onion, cilantro, or other additions. But this one—stewed tomatoes are the secret ingredient—never fails to inspire at least one guest to tell me it's the best guac he or she has ever had. • **MAKES ABOUT 2 CUPS**

2 ripe avocados (about 1 pound), peeled and pitted
½ cup stewed tomatoes (with their juices) (about ⅓ of a 14-ounce can)
2 cloves garlic, pressed through a garlic press or minced
2 tablespoons fresh lime juice, or more to taste
1 teaspoon coarse kosher salt, or more to taste
Tortilla chips, for serving

In a medium bowl, use a potato masher or fork to combine the avocados, stewed tomatoes (with their juices), garlic, lime juice, and salt. (You can prepare the guacamole up to 4 hours in advance, storing it in the refrigerator with a piece of plastic wrap directly on top of the guacamole, to prevent browning. If necessary, restir before serving.)

Taste, ideally with your wine, and add more lime juice and/or salt if you like. Serve the guacamole with the chips on the side.

making pink wine

You might think that Rosé wine is made simply by blending white and red wines. And in some cases, you'd be right.

But the better Rosés are made with an abbreviated red wine making process. After the grapes are crushed, rather than allowing the juices to ferment with the skins for as long as three or four weeks, extracting color, they let the juices run off after only a few days, extracting only a little color. The resulting pink wine will have mild red wine flavors, but with a best-served-cold, refreshing white wine lightness.

smoked paprika fried almonds

The hardest thing about making this recipe is finding blanched whole almonds, so I've suggested a few ideas for doing that below. But the effort is well worth it, because these easy-to-make nuts have a warm, haunting flavor that makes them absolutely, positively addictive! • **MAKES 3 CUPS**

1 tablespoon coarse kosher salt
2 teaspoons smoked paprika (see below)
¼ teaspoon cayenne pepper, optional
3 cups whole blanched raw almonds, preferably Marcona
   (about 1 pound) (see below)
¼ cup extra virgin olive oil

In a large bowl, combine the salt, paprika, and cayenne, if using. Set aside.

In a large skillet, combine the almonds and olive oil. Place the skillet over medium heat and cook, stirring occasionally, until the almonds are lightly browned, 4 to 7 minutes. Use a slotted spoon to transfer the nuts to the bowl with the salt mixture. Toss to thoroughly and evenly coat.

Allow the almonds to cool at least slightly before serving warm or at room temperature. (You can prepare the almonds up to a week in advance. Cool them thoroughly, then store them at room temperature in an airtight container.)

To blanch raw whole almonds: Place the almonds in a large heatproof bowl. Cover with 1 or 2 inches of rapidly boiling water, then let them sit for 2 minutes. Drain, then place the almonds inside a folded kitchen towel and rub them vigorously. Most of the skins should be loosened and can be easily slipped off with your fingers (it's tedious, but it works). Let the almonds dry completely before using them in this recipe.

NOTES Smoked paprika is without a doubt one of the best new ingredients—to us in the States at least—of the last five years. It's available in the spice section of most major supermarkets and at specialty food stores. Besides using it in this recipe, you can use it in Serrano Shrimp (page 123) and Spice-Rubbed Chicken Wings (page 152). You can also stir smoked paprika into salsas, soups, stews, and sauces—and sprinkle it over meats, poultry, and fish.

For blanched raw whole almonds, call around before you shop, and try the natural and specialty food stores in your area. You can also order them via Amazon.com or, even better, order whole blanched raw Marcona almonds, also available at Amazon.com. Marconas are round, flat Spanish almonds with a lovely soft texture, not unlike that of a cashew.

If you find whole Marcona almonds that have already been roasted and salted, you can use them, too. Just follow the same recipe, but cook them for only 3 or 4 minutes, until they're only slightly browned.

Finally, you can also blanch raw whole almonds easily at home (see above).

grilled pepper poppers

Here's a colorful take on the popular jalapeño popper appetizer, with all the fun of the original but without the breading and frying. This dish is a great way to kick off a backyard barbecue.

If you like, you can make the recipe your own by substituting a different herb—flat-leaf parsley and rosemary are both nice—or by adding some finely diced tomato to the cheese mixture. In all configurations, the peppers will be delicious with a chilled glass of Rosé. • SERVES 4 TO 6

One 8-ounce package cream cheese, room temperature
½ cup grated Parmesan cheese (2½ to 3 ounces)
¼ cup chopped fresh cilantro
¼ cup finely diced red onion
2 cloves garlic, pressed through a garlic press or minced
½ teaspoon coarse kosher salt
12 mini bell peppers, red, orange, yellow, green, or a combination, halved lengthwise, seeds and veins removed

In a medium bowl, combine the cream cheese, Parmesan cheese, cilantro, onion, garlic, and salt. Fill each pepper half with some of the cream cheese mixture (you might not need it all). (You can prepare the peppers up to a day in advance, storing them covered in the refrigerator.)

Prepare the grill to medium-high heat. Grill the peppers, filled side up, until blistered and slightly charred on the bottom, 3 to 5 minutes. Serve warm.

FOOD & WINE TIP Because of the richness of the filling in the peppers, this dish would also pair well either with Chardonnay, to complement that richness, or with Sauvignon Blanc or Pinot Grigio, to cut through it. If you decide to go with Sauvignon Blanc or Pinot Grigio, have a little lemon juice on hand and adjust the filling to work with your wine.

fig, goat cheese, and arugula salad with candied pecans

This recipe is inspired by one of my favorite restaurants in nearby Sonoma, the Girl and the Fig, where a similar dish is one of the signature items. • SERVES 6

¼ cup red wine vinegar
1 shallot, minced
2 teaspoons honey
½ teaspoon coarse kosher salt
½ teaspoon freshly ground black pepper
⅓ cup extra virgin olive oil
12 dried or 6 fresh figs, stems trimmed, quartered
12 cups loosely packed arugula (about 6 ounces)
¾ cup crumbled goat cheese (about 3½ ounces)
¾ cup candied pecans, homemade (recipe follows) or store-bought

■ In a small bowl, combine the vinegar, shallot, honey, salt, and pepper, whisking to dissolve the salt. Whisk in the olive oil. Set aside. (You can prepare the dressing up to 3 days in advance, storing it covered in the refrigerator. Return to room temperature before proceeding.)

■ In another small bowl, combine the figs with about 2 tablespoons of the dressing. In a large bowl, combine the arugula, cheese, and the remaining dressing to taste. Transfer the salad to a serving bowl or platter, or to individual plates, dividing it evenly. Arrange the figs and pecans on top and serve.

homemade candied pecans • *Makes about 2 cups*

Of course you can buy candied nuts at the supermarket, but they'll never taste as good as homemade.

2 cups raw pecans (about 7 ounces)
¼ cup dark corn syrup
2 tablespoons sugar
2 teaspoons coarse kosher salt

Preheat the oven to 325°F. Spray a rimmed baking sheet with nonstick cooking spray. In a medium bowl, combine the pecans, corn syrup, sugar, and salt, tossing to thoroughly and evenly coat the nuts. Spread the nut mixture onto the prepared baking sheet in a single layer. Bake until the nuts are browned and the sugar mixture is bubbling, about 18 minutes, stirring halfway through. Transfer the baking sheet to a wire rack and cool completely. (You can prepare the nuts up to a week in advance, storing them at room temperature in an airtight container.)

mediterranean meze plate

This recipe is Mediterranean refreshment on a plate, and beautifully complemented by fruity, refreshing Rosé. • **SERVES 8**

2 rounds pita bread, white, whole wheat, or a combination
3 tablespoons extra virgin olive oil, divided
About 4 cups Tabbouleh (recipe follows)
About 2 cups Hummus (recipe follows)
24 kalamata olives

▓ Preheat the oven to 375°F.

▓ Cut the pitas in half. Split each half into two semicircles, then cut each semicircle into 4 wedges. Arrange the pita wedges on a baking sheet, smooth side down, and brush with 2 tablespoons of the olive oil. Bake until lightly toasted, 10 to 12 minutes. Set aside to cool.

▓ Arrange the pita toasts, tabbouleh, hummus, and olives on individual plates, dividing them evenly. Drizzle the remaining 1 tablespoon of olive oil over the hummus and serve.

tabbouleh · *Makes about 4 cups*

This Middle Eastern grain salad is an ideal picnic food and is always welcome at a potluck.

2 tablespoons fresh lemon juice, or more to taste
1 teaspoon coarse kosher salt, or more to taste
½ teaspoon freshly ground black pepper, or more to taste
¼ cup extra virgin olive oil
¾ cup bulgur wheat (see below)
1 tomato, cut into ¼-inch dice
½ cucumber, peeled and cut into ¼-inch dice
¼ red onion, cut into ¼-inch dice
⅓ cup coarsely chopped fresh flat-leaf parsley
⅓ cup coarsely chopped fresh mint

In a small bowl, combine the lemon juice, salt, and pepper, whisking to dissolve the salt. Whisk in the olive oil. Set aside. (You can prepare the dressing up to 3 days in advance, storing it covered in the refrigerator. Return to room temperature before using.)

In a large bowl, combine the bulgur wheat and 1 cup of boiling water. Cover and set aside for 30 minutes.

Add the tomato, cucumber, onion, parsley, and mint to the bulgur mixture. Add the dressing and toss gently. Taste, ideally with your wine, and add more lemon juice, salt, and/or pepper if you like.

hummus · *Makes about 2 cups*

Hummus is most often served with pita. But it's also great as a vegetable dip or sandwich spread.

One 19-ounce can chickpeas (garbanzo beans)
½ cup tahini (see below)
6 tablespoons fresh lemon juice (from 2 or 3 lemons), or more to taste
2 tablespoons extra virgin olive oil
2 cloves garlic
1 teaspoon coarse kosher salt, or more to taste
⅛ teaspoon cayenne pepper

Drain the chickpeas, reserving their liquid.

In the bowl of a food processor, combine the chickpeas, tahini, lemon juice, olive oil, garlic, salt, cayenne, and 2 tablespoons of the reserved chickpea liquid and process until very smooth, scraping down the bowl as necessary. Add more reserved liquid as needed. Taste, ideally with your wine, and add more lemon juice and/or salt if you like. (You can prepare the hummus up to 3 days in advance, storing it covered in the refrigerator. Return to room temperature before serving.)

NOTES Bulgur wheat is available in the bulk section of many major supermarkets and at natural food stores. Besides using it in this recipe, you can use it in other grain dishes and Mediterranean recipes.

Tahini is a peanut butter–like paste made of ground sesame seeds. It's available in the ethnic or health food section of most major supermarkets and at natural foods stores. Besides using it in this recipe, you can use it in Lamb Meatballs with Mint, Pine Nuts, and Tahini Sauce (page 126); in other Middle Eastern dishes; and in sauces and spreads.

mini pesto burgers

If they haven't hit your area yet, they're on the way—mini burgers, often called sliders, are all the rage at restaurants here in the San Francisco Bay Area. It's Americana meets small plates mania. What's not to like? • SERVES 6

¾ cup loosely packed fresh basil leaves
¼ cup grated Parmesan cheese (about 1½ ounces)
2 tablespoons pine nuts, toasted (see page 26)
1 clove garlic
2 teaspoons coarse kosher salt, divided
¾ teaspoon freshly ground black pepper, divided
¼ cup extra virgin olive oil
1 pound 85 percent lean ground beef
6 slices provolone cheese
1 tomato, cut into 6 slices
6 white, whole wheat, or sourdough dinner rolls, split horizontally

▓ In the bowl of a food processor, combine the basil, Parmesan cheese, pine nuts, garlic, ½ teaspoon of the salt, and ¼ teaspoon of the pepper and pulse to finely chop, scraping down the bowl as necessary. With the motor running, slowly add the olive oil and process until smooth, scraping down the bowl as necessary. Set the pesto aside. (You can prepare the pesto in advance, storing it covered in the refrigerator for up to a week or in the freezer for several months. Thaw in the refrigerator before proceeding.)

▓ Shape the beef into 6 patties, about 3 inches in diameter and ½ inch thick. Cut the provolone cheese slices so that they're 2½ inches in diameter. (You can shape the patties and cut the cheese up to 2 days in advance, storing them covered in the refrigerator.)

▓ Prepare the grill to medium-high heat and lightly oil the grate. Sprinkle both sides of the patties with the remaining 1½ teaspoons of salt and ½ teaspoon of pepper.

▓ Grill the patties to desired doneness, about 3 minutes per side for medium. During the last minute, place a slice of provolone cheese on top of each patty and place the rolls cut side down on the grill, to melt the cheese and lightly toast the buns.

▓ Place the tomato slices on the bottom halves of the rolls. Top with the patties, pesto, and the top halves of the rolls and serve.

FOOD & WINE TIP These burgers are also great with Pinot Noir and with Zinfandel.

grilled gazpacho shooters

Gazpacho is a celebration of summer in a cup, and is best enjoyed when tomatoes and peppers are at their just-picked peak of flavor. If you can, buy them at the local farmer's market.

Instead of serving the soup as a shooter, you can also serve it as a first course. In that case, double the recipe for six one-cup servings.

- **MAKES 12 SHOOTERS (¼ CUP EACH)**

1 red onion
4 plum tomatoes, halved lengthwise and seeded
2 red bell peppers, quartered, cored, and seeded
1½ teaspoons coarse kosher salt, or more to taste
½ teaspoon freshly ground black pepper, or more to taste
5 tablespoons extra virgin olive oil, divided
4 teaspoons sherry vinegar, or more to taste
¼ teaspoon hot sauce, such as Tabasco, or more to taste
Twelve ⅛-inch-thick slices peeled cucumber

Keeping the root end intact, cut the onion into 12 wedges.

Prepare the grill to medium-high heat. In a large bowl, toss the onion, tomatoes, red peppers, salt, pepper, and 1 tablespoon of the olive oil. Grill the tomatoes skin side down until softened and lightly charred, about 2 minutes. Grill the red peppers and onion until softened and lightly charred, 4 to 5 minutes per side. As each vegetable is done, return it to the bowl.

In a blender or food processor, combine the grilled vegetables and their accumulated juices with 2 tablespoons of the remaining olive oil and ¾ cup of water. Process until very smooth, scraping down the bowl as necessary (you may have to do this in batches). Transfer the soup to a container and chill for at least 2 hours. (You can prepare the gazpacho up to 3 days in advance, storing it covered in the refrigerator.)

Stir in the vinegar and hot sauce. Taste, ideally with your wine, and add more vinegar, hot sauce, salt, and/or pepper if you like. Serve the soup chilled, each serving garnished with ½ teaspoon of the remaining olive oil and a slice of cucumber.

barbecued chicken pizza

Every few months, I get together with a group of friends to have a wine-tasting party. It's a pretty casual affair—we rotate hosting, the host chooses the theme (maybe a wine varietal or region, or wines to go with a specific dish) and makes a few snacks, and the rest of the group brings wines that fit the theme. I highly recommend it as an easy and affordable way to get to know and appreciate both wines and friends.

Our inaugural gathering was at my house and, perhaps not surprisingly since it's my favorite wine, featured Rosé. This recipe was among the snacks I prepared. And while the good company is definitely what inspired us to continue our get-togethers, I'm sure the pizza didn't hurt. • **SERVES 4 TO 8**

One 12-ounce pizza dough, homemade or store-bought
¼ cup bottled barbecue sauce
1 small cooked chicken breast, shredded into bite-sized pieces
  (you should have about 1½ cups)
1 cup shredded Monterey Jack cheese (about 4 ounces)
¼ red onion, thinly sliced
2 scallions, white and light green parts only, thinly sliced on a
  diagonal
½ teaspoon coarse kosher salt
3 tablespoons coarsely chopped fresh cilantro

▦ Preheat the oven, along with a pizza stone if you have one, to 500°F.

▦ On a lightly floured surface, roll or stretch the dough out to a 12- to 14-inch round. Transfer the dough to a pizza pan or a flour- or cornmeal-dusted pizza paddle. Top with the barbecue sauce, chicken, cheese, onion, scallions, and salt. Transfer the pizza to the oven and bake for 10 to 12 minutes, until the pizza is golden and crisp.

▦ Sprinkle the pizza with the cilantro, cut into wedges, and serve.

buffalo drumettes with cool blue cheese dipping sauce

The genius combination of hot sauce and blue cheese dressing was invented in Buffalo, New York's Anchor Bar. The two flavors are so on opposite ends of the spectrum, but so amazingly complementary. Adding another dimension to the combination, a glass of Rosé is a fruity, calming presence in a smoldering mouth.

The most authentic way to cook the wings is to fry them. But to me, baking is just as good and much less messy. If you prefer to fry the wings, those instructions are below as well. • **SERVES 6**

¾ cup sour cream
⅔ cup crumbled blue cheese (about 3 ounces)
¼ cup mayonnaise
18 chicken wing drumettes (see below)
3 tablespoons safflower, sunflower, peanut, or other high-heat cooking oil
6 tablespoons (¾ stick) unsalted butter, melted
2 tablespoons hot sauce, such as Tabasco
1 teaspoon coarse kosher salt
6 celery ribs, cut crosswise in halves or thirds, then lengthwise into sticks

▓ In a medium bowl, combine the sour cream, cheese, and mayonnaise. (You can prepare the dipping sauce up to 3 days in advance, storing it covered in the refrigerator.)

▓ Preheat the oven to 425°F.

▓ In a large bowl, toss the drumettes with the oil. Arrange the chicken on a rimmed baking sheet and bake until cooked through, 30 to 35 minutes, turning halfway through.

▓ (You can also deep-fry the drumettes. Substitute the 3 tablespoons of oil with 4 or 5 cups of canola, grapeseed, or other neutral-flavored oil, adding enough to a large, heavy stockpot so that the oil is 1 inch deep. Place the stockpot over medium heat and warm the oil to 370°F. Prepare a paper towel-lined platter or baking sheet. Add the drumettes, 6 at a time, to the hot oil and cook, turning occasionally, until cooked through, golden, and crisp, 6 to 8 minutes. Use tongs or a slotted spoon to transfer the cooked drumettes to the prepared platter. While you're cooking, adjust the heat as necessary to maintain the temperature.)

Meanwhile, in another large bowl, combine the butter, hot sauce, and salt, whisking to dissolve the salt.

Add the cooked drumettes to the butter mixture, tossing to coat. Serve the drumettes warm or at room temperature with the blue cheese sauce and celery sticks on the side.

NOTE If you can't find drumettes, you can buy 9 or 18 whole chicken wings. Use poultry shears or a sharp knife to cut off the wing tips (discard them or save them for another use), then halve the wings at the joint. Use both remaining pieces of the 9 wings, or use just the drumettes of the 18 wings (discard or save the other pieces for another use).

FOOD & WINE TIP These wings are purposefully not as hot as ones you might get in a restaurant—too much heat just overpowers the wine. Also, because of the heat, these wings will be best with an off-dry, or slightly sweet, Rosé. If you don't know if your Rosé is dry or off-dry—the label might provide some clues, but not always—don't worry about it.

pinot noir

Pinot Noir has experienced explosive growth over the past few years, largely because of the movie *Sideways*. In it, several characters wax poetic about Pinot Noir, and they're not alone. Many believe that when Pinot Noir is good, wine doesn't get any better.

Pinot Noir, however, is notoriously fickle and can come in a wide array of flavors and styles. It can be super-fruity, chock full of cherry, raspberry, and strawberry flavors. It can have notes of lavender or roses. And it can also be more vegetal or earthy.

What you can pretty much always count on, though, are red fruits, soft tannins, and, generally, a lighter body compared to other red wines. All of which makes Pinot Noir a great bridge wine, somewhere between the crispness of a white and the intensity of a big, bold red—and perfect for all the foods that fall in between.

pinot noir by another name

• *Burgundy, Red Burgundy.* As with other French wines, these French Pinot Noirs are labeled with the name of the area they're from. They might have the general area name Burgundy, or names of subregions within Burgundy (Côte d'Or, for example). Basically, any red wine from Burgundy, with the exception of those from Beaujolais, will be made from the Pinot Noir grape.

pairing with pinot noir

Although there are, of course, nuances to Pinot Noir, the most important factors in food and wine pairing aren't a wine's nuances, but its broad strokes. If you learn a wine's overall characteristics and combine that information with the General Pairing Tips (page 6), you'll have a near-perfect pairing every time.

Broad characteristics:
- dry (not sweet)
- medium in acidity, crispness, or brightness
- medium-low to medium in tannins
- medium weight
- medium intensity

Pairs well with dishes that are:

- not sweet
- medium in acidity, crispness, or brightness
- medium-low to medium in richness/meatiness/heaviness, acidity, or slight bitterness
- medium weight
- medium intensity

For example, grilled salmon, turkey with gravy, or roast mushrooms.

Another way to think of Pinot Noir is, pair it with foods that are too meaty for a white wine, but too light for a bigger red wine.

fine-tuning

With Pinot Noir, it never hurts to add some earthy element to the food. Mushrooms, cured olives, woody herbs like rosemary or thyme, and earthy, dusty spices like paprika, fennel, and cumin—all of these will help seal the deal.

And as with other wines, acid and salt continue to be important. But as the wines get darker, so do the acids that best complement them. For Pinot Noir, think red wine vinegar, sherry vinegar, and if the rest of the dish is bright enough, even balsamic vinegar.

other nuances

Once you have a pairing that's working on the basis of sweetness, acidity, tannins, weight, and intensity, you can start playing with subtler nuances.

In addition to the earthiness mentioned above, some of the subtle flavors that you might find in a Pinot Noir include red berries (especially raspberries, strawberries, and cranberries), blackberries, cherries, pomegranate, herbs, and licorice. So it works to add those flavors, or foods that complement them, to your dishes.

other thoughts

Some foods that are considered classic pairings with Pinot Noir are salmon, tuna, mushrooms and mushroom sauces, poultry (especially duck), lamb, veal, pork, and beef (especially lean and/or rare).

crushed fennel crackers

Sure. You could buy crackers at the supermarket. But those store-bought crackers won't feature fennel, which so beautifully marries to the often herby nature of Pinot Noir. And they won't have the delicious bursts of salt, which will bring out the wine's fruit. Most importantly, they won't be lovingly homemade—a quality which often adds the best flavors of all. • **MAKES ABOUT 40 CRACKERS**

2 tablespoons whole fennel seeds
1 cup all-purpose flour, plus more for the work surface
¾ cup whole wheat flour
1¾ teaspoons coarse kosher salt
3 tablespoons extra virgin olive oil
3 tablespoons Pinot Noir, or other dry red wine
¾ teaspoon coarse fleur de sel, other coarse finishing salt, or coarse kosher salt

▓ Preheat the oven to 450°F.

▓ Use a mortar and pestle to lightly crush the fennel seeds. (If you don't have a mortar and pestle, place them in a small bowl and lightly crush them with the end of a wooden spoon.) Set aside.

▓ In a medium bowl, combine the flours and the kosher salt. Add the olive oil and ½ cup of water, working the mixture with a spoon or your fingers until it becomes a soft, crumbly ball. Press the dough together, gathering up any stray flour.

▓ Transfer the dough to a lightly floured work surface and divide it in thirds. Working with one third at a time (keep the remaining pieces covered with plastic wrap), pat the dough into a square, then roll it into a rectangle about ¹⁄₁₆ inch thick, 8 inches wide, and 14 inches long, sprinkling a little flour under the dough as needed.

▓ Use a pastry brush to lightly brush the dough with some of the wine. Sprinkle on about ⅓ of the fennel and ¼ teaspoon of the fleur de sel. Cut the dough in half lengthwise, then crosswise into 2-inch slices, making 12 to 14 roughly 2 x 4-inch crackers. (Don't bother to trim the rough edges—they add a nice rustic character.) Carefully transfer the crackers to a rimmed baking sheet and bake until nicely browned, 9 to 11 minutes. Transfer the baking sheet to a wire rack and let the crackers cool completely. As each batch bakes, repeat with the next piece of dough, making 3 batches of crackers in all. (You can prepare the crackers up to a week in advance, storing them at room temperature in an airtight container.)

olive bread toasts with teleme cheese

These simple but full-flavored toasts feature soft, creamy Teleme cheese complemented by olives, rosemary, and garlic.

Teleme is kind of like a Brie without the washed rind. You can find it at cheese shops and better supermarkets—or substitute Port-Salut, which is similar in taste and texture. • **MAKES 16 TOASTS**

16 small, thin slices artisan olive bread, toasted (see page 13)
2 cloves garlic, cut in half crosswise
8 ounces Teleme cheese (see above), cut into ¼-inch slices
2 teaspoons chopped fresh rosemary
8 oil-cured black olives, pitted and halved

▒ Preheat the oven to 400°F.

▒ Rub one side of each toast with the cut sides of the garlic. Top the garlic-rubbed side of the toasts with the cheese, cutting the cheese as necessary to make it fit on the bread. Arrange the toasts on a rimmed baking sheet, sprinkle with the rosemary, and top with the olive halves, dividing them evenly. Bake until the cheese is warm and melted, 4 to 5 minutes. Serve warm.

enter tannins

As we get into the red wines, tannins start to become a factor in food and wine pairing. Tannins are the compounds that can give you that dry-mouth sensation in a wine, usually accompanied by some bitterness. Tannins occur naturally in the skin of grapes, even white grapes. But in most white wine–making, the juice is fermented without the skins and so it doesn't pick up the tannins. (Tannins can also come from oak aging—that is, aging the wine in contact with some form of oak—so some white wines do have a little.)

Because of the bitterness, you might think tannins are a bad thing. Not so. Good tannins help give a wine the ability to develop character as it ages, along with adding structure and interest. And they soften over time.

Throughout the red wine chapters, as the wines get more tannic, per General Pairing Tip 3 (page 6), we'll start using rich/meaty/heavy and bitter elements in the recipes. Also, our wines will get more intense, so per General Pairing Tip 5 (page 7), our food will become more intense as well. And just as acid and salt have been important elements in food to balance and even soften acidic wines, per Fine Tuning Tip 1 (page 8), they'll be important elements to balance and even soften tannic wines.

mushroom brie puff pastry bites

Pinot Noir is often described as mushroom-y—its aromas can be earthy, damp, and just the slightest bit funky, like those of mushrooms. So it's no surprise that mushrooms complement Pinot Noir so well.

Here, subtly mushroom-flavored Brie is combined with rich, crisp puff pastry for an easy yet elegant appetizer. • **MAKES 24**

4 ounces mushroom Brie cheese (see below)
1 sheet (half of a 17.3-ounce package) puff pastry, thawed
1 tablespoon Dijon, stone-ground, or other good-quality mustard
Special equipment: one 24-muffin mini (1¾-inch) muffin pan
  or two 12-muffin mini (1¾-inch) muffin pans

▓ Cut the cheese into 24 chunks, each about ¾ x ¾ x ½ inches. Arrange the cheese on a parchment- or plastic wrap-lined plate or baking sheet and freeze for at least an hour. (You can freeze the cheese, covered, for up to a week.)

▓ Preheat the oven to 425°F.

▓ On a lightly floured work surface, roll the pastry out to a 12 x 18-inch rectangle. Use a fork to pierce the pastry all over. Cut the pastry into 6 pieces widthwise, then 4 pieces lengthwise, making 24 pieces, each 3 inches square. Gently arrange a square in each section of one or two mini muffin pans, pressing them into the sides and bottoms of the cups. Dab ⅛ teaspoon of mustard onto each square, then top each with a piece of cheese. Bake until golden brown, about 12 minutes. Let cool 1 or 2 minutes before serving warm.

> **NOTE** Mushroom Brie is available at cheese shops and specialty food stores, and in the specialty cheese section of most major supermarkets. If you can't find it, ask your cheese shop to order it for you, or substitute regular Brie and top each baked pastry bite with a drop of truffle oil, available at better supermarkets and specialty food stores.

FOOD & WINE TIP The rich, elegant nature of this dish also makes it a great candidate to pair with sparkling wine—especially a dry, or brut, sparkler.

grilled vegetable ratatouille

Traditionally, ratatouille is made by simmering a summery blend of vegetables in olive oil. But in this recipe, we're cooking the veggies on the grill, which gives it a touch of fire-roasted flavor. Also atypically, this version includes mushrooms, which help marry the ratatouille to the wine.

Enjoy any leftover ratatouille as a side dish, a relish, or a topping for a grilled steak, lamb chop, or chicken breast. • **MAKES ABOUT 4 CUPS**

1 red onion
4 plum tomatoes, halved lengthwise and seeded
2 zucchini, quartered lengthwise
1 Japanese eggplant, quartered lengthwise
1 red bell pepper, cored, seeded, and cut into 1-inch strips
½ portobello mushroom, trimmed and halved again
2 teaspoons coarse kosher salt, or more to taste
1 teaspoon freshly ground black pepper, or more to taste
6 tablespoons extra virgin olive oil, divided
1 tablespoon red wine vinegar, or more to taste
1 tablespoon chopped fresh basil
1 tablespoon chopped fresh thyme
1½ teaspoons chopped fresh marjoram
Stone-ground crackers, for serving

▨ Keeping the root end intact, cut the onion into 12 wedges.

▨ Prepare the grill to medium-high heat. In a large bowl, toss the onion, tomatoes, zucchini, eggplant, red pepper, mushroom, salt, pepper, and 2 tablespoons of the olive oil. Grill the tomatoes skin side down until softened and lightly charred, about 2 minutes. Grill the onion, zucchini, eggplant, red pepper, and mushroom until softened and lightly charred, 4 to 5 minutes per side.

▨ Once the vegetables are cool enough to handle, in the bowl of a food processor, combine the tomatoes, vinegar, and remaining ¼ cup of olive oil and pulse to form a chunky sauce, scraping down the bowl as necessary. Transfer the sauce to a large bowl. Cut the remaining grilled vegetables into ½-inch dice and add them. Stir in the basil, thyme, and marjoram. (You can prepare the ratatouille up to 2 days in advance, storing it covered in the refrigerator. Return to room temperature or reheat it slightly before serving.)

▨ Taste, ideally with your wine, and add more vinegar, salt, and/or pepper if you like. Serve the ratatouille warm or at room temperature with the crackers on the side.

grilled tuna niçoise

With a brief cook on the grill, the dish gets just enough dark flavor to merit a light red. • **SERVES 6**

1 tablespoon red wine vinegar
1½ teaspoons Dijon mustard
1 clove garlic, pressed through a garlic press or minced
1¼ teaspoons coarse kosher salt, divided
¾ plus ⅛ teaspoon freshly ground black pepper, divided
⅓ cup plus 3 tablespoons extra virgin olive oil, divided
9 small red potatoes (about 12 ounces), halved
18 to 24 haricots verts (thin French green beans) (about 3 ounces)
18 cherry tomatoes, ideally a mix of colors and shapes
1 pound raw tuna steaks, about 1½ inches thick
18 niçoise olives, or other good-quality black olives
Special equipment: skewers, soaked in water for at least 10 minutes
   if they're wood or bamboo, and a small grill basket

▨ In a small bowl, combine the vinegar, mustard, garlic, ¼ teaspoon of the salt, and ⅛ teaspoon of the pepper, whisking to dissolve the salt. Whisk in ⅓ cup of the olive oil. Set aside. (You can prepare the dressing up to 3 days in advance, storing it covered in the refrigerator. Return to room temperature before serving.)

▨ Place the potatoes in a medium saucepan of cold well-salted water (1 tablespoon of coarse kosher salt per quart). Bring to a boil over high heat and cook, stirring occasionally, until the potatoes are tender, about 3 minutes. Use a slotted spoon to transfer the potatoes to a paper towel-lined bowl or plate. Set aside. Add the haricots verts to the saucepan and cook, stirring occasionally, until tender, 1½ to 2 minutes. Drain the haricots verts and transfer them to the plate with the potatoes. (You can prepare the potatoes and haricots verts up to 4 hours in advance. Cool them, then store them covered in the refrigerator.)

▨ Thread the potatoes onto skewers and arrange the haricots verts in a small grill basket. Thread the tomatoes onto skewers.

▨ Prepare the grill to high heat. Brush the potatoes, haricots verts, tomatoes, and tuna with the remaining 3 tablespoons of olive oil. Sprinkle with the remaining 1 teaspoon of salt and ¾ teaspoon of pepper. Grill the tuna until well seared, about 2 minutes per side for rare. Grill the potatoes and haricots verts until lightly charred, about 2 minutes per side. Grill the tomatoes until lightly charred, about 1½ minutes per side.

▨ Cut the tuna into ½-inch slices and arrange it on a platter or on individual plates. Arrange the potatoes, haricots verts, tomatoes, and olives around the tuna. Drizzle the dressing on top and serve.

mushroom sherry soup

This is an especially fragrant and luxurious soup, one that's both hearty and delicate at the same time. In addition to the sherry, it's finished with a little crème fraîche, which adds both a silky texture and a delicious tang. • SERVES 6

2 tablespoons unsalted butter
2 tablespoons extra virgin olive oil
1 onion, cut into ½-inch dice
4 cloves garlic, pressed through a garlic press or minced
8 ounces brown, cremini, or portobello mushrooms, or a combination, trimmed and thinly sliced (you should have about 4 cups)
4 ounces shiitake mushrooms, stems removed, thinly sliced (you should have about 3 cups)
1½ teaspoons coarse kosher salt, or more to taste
½ teaspoon freshly ground black pepper, or more to taste
2 tablespoons plus 1 teaspoon fresh thyme leaves, divided
5 cups reduced-sodium chicken broth
3 tablespoons dry sherry
2 tablespoons crème fraîche, homemade or store-bought
1 tablespoon soy sauce

▓ In a large stockpot over medium-high heat, warm the butter and olive oil until the butter is melted. Add the onion and cook, stirring occasionally, until it begins to brown, about 4 minutes. Stir in the garlic and cook until fragrant, about 1 minute. Add the mushrooms, salt, pepper, and 2 tablespoons of the thyme, and cook until the mushrooms become limp, 2 to 4 minutes. Add the broth, scraping up any browned bits on the bottom of the pot. Bring to a boil, reduce to a simmer, and cook, stirring occasionally, until the mushrooms are tender, 7 to 10 minutes. Turn off the heat and let the liquid cool slightly.

▓ Transfer about half of the soup to a blender or food processor and puree, scraping down the jar or bowl as necessary. Return the mixture to the pot and stir in the sherry, crème fraîche, and soy sauce. (You can prepare the soup up to 3 days in advance. Cool it, then store it covered in the refrigerator.)

▓ If necessary, gently reheat the soup. Taste, ideally with your wine, and add more salt and/or pepper if you like. Serve hot, garnished with the remaining 1 teaspoon of thyme.

roast beef carpaccio with roast-ed red peppers and arugula

Technically, carpaccio is thin slices of raw beef, but restaurants the world over have adopted the word to apply to thin slices of pretty much anything, from smoked salmon to prosciutto, and even thin slices of vegetables like fennel or beets.

Here, we're using roast beef. One, because it's readily available and relatively inexpensive. And two, because it has a natural affinity to the wine. • SERVES 4

3 tablespoons extra virgin olive oil
1 tablespoon balsamic vinegar
½ teaspoon coarse kosher salt
¼ teaspoon freshly ground black pepper, plus more for sprinkling
3 cups loosely packed arugula (about 1½ ounces)
⅓ cup drained roasted red peppers, diced
12 thin slices rare roast beef (6 to 8 ounces)

▨ In a small bowl, combine the olive oil, vinegar, salt, and pepper, whisking to dissolve the salt. (You can prepare the dressing up to 3 days in advance, storing it covered in the refrigerator. Return to room temperature before proceeding.)

▨ In a medium bowl, toss the arugula and roasted red peppers with about ⅔ of the dressing. Set aside.

▨ Arrange the roast beef slices, slightly overlapping, on individual plates, dividing the slices evenly. Drizzle with the remaining olive oil mixture, dividing it evenly. Mound some of the arugula mixture in the center of each plate, sprinkle or grind a little fresh pepper on top, and serve.

FOOD & WINE TIP The dressing in this dish is purposefully on the mild side. Too much acidity can make a relatively low-tannin wine, like Pinot Noir, taste sour.

serrano shrimp

Serrano ham is to Spain what prosciutto is to Italy—they're both cured ham, but Serrano ham has a more savory, deep, richly meaty flavor. You can find it in the deli section of better supermarkets and specialty stores. But if you can't find it, substitute prosciutto. Either way, the dish is delish. • **SERVES 4 TO 6**

¾ cup sour cream
1 tablespoon fresh lemon juice
1 teaspoon smoked paprika (see note on page 100)
8 to 12 thin slices Serrano ham (see above), each slice cut
    lengthwise into 2 to 3 strips (you should have at least 24 pieces)
24 large raw, peeled shrimp (about 1 pound)
3 tablespoons extra virgin olive oil

▓ In a small bowl, whisk together the sour cream, lemon juice, and paprika. Set aside. (You can prepare the sauce up to 2 days in advance, storing it covered in the refrigerator.)

▓ Wrap a piece of Serrano ham around each shrimp, from head to tail end, as if you are bandaging it. Set the shrimp aside. (You can wrap the shrimp up to 4 hours in advance, storing them covered in the refrigerator.)

▓ In a large skillet over medium-high heat, warm the olive oil. Add the shrimp in a single layer and cook until the ham starts to crisp and the shrimp are just cooked through, 1 to 2 minutes per side (you may have to do this in batches).

▓ Meanwhile, drizzle the sour cream mixture decoratively onto a platter or onto individual plates, dividing it evenly.

▓ Arrange the shrimp on top of the sour cream mixture. Serve hot, with forks or toothpicks for spearing the shrimp.

herbes de provence salmon skewers with provençal aïoli

Herbes de Provence is a wonderful mixture of dried herbs evocative of southern France. Most blends include basil, rosemary, sage, marjoram, and thyme—but, to me, the best ones also have lavender. It adds a slight flowery perfume that balances the more rustic herbs.

Look for herbes de Provence in the spice section of most major supermarkets or at specialty food stores. It's often packaged in a small clay crock. Besides using it in this recipe, you can use herbes de Provence in White Cheddar with Wine-Soaked Cherries and Herbs (page 133). It's also great sprinkled on roasting poultry, pork, and lamb and stirred into a summer tomato pasta. • **SERVES 6**

¾ cup mayonnaise
24 capers, finely chopped (you should have about 2 teaspoons), plus 1 teaspoon packing liquid
4 cloves garlic, pressed through a garlic press or minced
¼ cup extra virgin olive oil, divided
1½ pounds salmon fillets, cut on a diagonal into ½-inch strips (you should have about 18 pieces)
2 teaspoons herbes de Provence (see above)
½ teaspoon coarse kosher salt
½ teaspoon freshly ground black pepper
Special equipment: about eighteen 8-inch skewers, soaked in water for at least 10 minutes if they're wood or bamboo

▒ In a small bowl, whisk together the mayonnaise, capers, caper packing liquid, garlic, and 1 tablespoon of the olive oil. Set aside. (You can prepare the aïoli up to a day in advance, storing it covered in the refrigerator.)

▒ Thread the salmon onto skewers, one strip per skewer. Brush both sides with the remaining 3 tablespoons of olive oil and sprinkle with the herbes de Provence, salt, and pepper.

▒ Prepare the grill to medium-high heat. Grill the salmon until it's cooked through, 1½ to 2 minutes per side. Serve the salmon with the aïoli on the side.

FOOD & WINE TIP Red wine with fish? Absolutely. In fact, Pinot Noir and salmon, in almost any incarnation, is considered one of the all-time great food and wine pairings.

lamb meatballs with mint, pine nuts, and tahini sauce

Pinot Noir is a natural choice for lamb, especially in a lighter preparation like these minty meatballs. The tahini counters the brightness with a slightly earthy and decidedly Middle Eastern spin, solidifying the match. • **MAKES ABOUT 20 MEATBALLS WITH SAUCE**

6 tablespoons tahini (see note on page 105)
3 tablespoons extra virgin olive oil
¼ cup fresh lemon juice (from about 2 lemons)
2 cloves garlic, pressed through a garlic press or minced
2¾ teaspoons coarse kosher salt, divided, or more to taste
1 large egg
½ cup panko (Japanese-style breadcrumbs)
¼ cup pine nuts, toasted (see page 26)
3 scallions, white and light green parts only, thinly sliced
1 teaspoon freshly ground black pepper, or more to taste
3 tablespoons plus 1½ teaspoons chopped fresh mint, divided
1 pound ground lamb

In a small bowl, combine 3 tablespoons of water with the tahini, olive oil, lemon juice, garlic, and ¼ teaspoon of the salt, whisking to dissolve the salt. (You can prepare the tahini sauce up to 3 days in advance, storing it covered in the refrigerator. Return to room temperature before serving.)

In a large bowl, whisk together the egg, panko, pine nuts, scallions, pepper, 3 tablespoons of the mint, and the remaining 2½ teaspoons of salt. Add the lamb and gently mix until well combined. With dampened hands, shape the mixture into about 20 meatballs, 1½ inches in diameter. (You can shape the meatballs up to a day in advance, storing them covered in the refrigerator. Return to room temperature before proceeding.)

Preheat the broiler and arrange a rack about 6 inches from the heat.

Transfer the meatballs to a foil-lined baking sheet. Broil the meatballs until cooked through and lightly browned, 8 to 10 minutes, turning halfway through.

Pool the tahini sauce on a platter or on individual plates, dividing it evenly. Arrange the meatballs on top and sprinkle with the remaining 1½ teaspoons of mint. Taste a meatball with some sauce, ideally with your wine, and sprinkle with more salt and/or pepper if you like. Serve hot, with forks or toothpicks for spearing the meatballs.

merlot

f Pinot Noir gained acclaim via the movie *Sideways*, Merlot lost it. Merlot drinkers were scorned, like Chardonnay drinkers can be, simply because they drink what's popular.

But Merlot is popular for good reason. Like Chardonnay, Merlot can be big and rich, but also fruity and soft, without being overly high in acids or tannins—which makes Merlot easy to drink and easy to pair with food.

If that doesn't spark your interest in Merlot, maybe this will. You know all those famous red wines from Bordeaux? Those wines that are considered some of the best in the world? Well, they're all blended with Merlot. And most are mostly Merlot.

merlot by another name

• *Bordeaux, Red Bordeaux*. As with other French wines, these French Merlot blends are labeled with the name of the area they're from. They might have the general name Bordeaux, or the names of subregions within Bordeaux (Pomerol, for example). In blends from the Left Bank of Bordeaux, Cabernet will be the dominant grape, followed by Merlot. On the Right Bank, Merlot dominates.

• *Meritage.* A group of American vintners have trademarked this name, pronounced to rhyme with "heritage," for Bordeaux-style blends made in the United States. These wines often include Merlot but may or may not be mostly Merlot.

pairing with merlot

Although there are, of course, nuances to Merlot, the most important factors in food and wine pairing aren't a wine's nuances, but its broad strokes. If you learn a wine's overall characteristics and combine that information with the General Pairing Tips (page 6), you'll have a near-perfect pairing every time.

Broad characteristics:
• dry (not sweet)
• medium in acidity, crispness, or brightness
• medium in tannins
• medium to heavy weight
• medium to strong intensity

Pairs well with dishes that are:

- not sweet
- medium in acidity, crispness, or brightness
- medium in richness/meatiness/heaviness, acidity, or slight bitterness
- medium to heavy weight
- medium to strong intensity

For example, duck with plum sauce, lamb stew, or mushroom risotto.

fine-tuning

Salt and acid continue to be important tools. But as the fruit flavors in the wines get darker—blackberries in Merlot as opposed to raspberries and cherries in Pinot Noir—so do the acids that best complement them. This means that with Merlot, balsamic vinegar is your best friend.

Because Merlot is a very fruity wine, it can also pair well with foods that have a fruity element, especially dark fruit. But remember that adding fruit can add sweetness, making your wine taste sour. So either balance the sweetness with acid, or add fruitiness without adding sweetness—by using fruit zest, fruit-infused vinegars and oils, or even dried fruits, which tend to be less sweet than their fresh counterparts.

other nuances

Once you have a pairing that's working on the basis of sweetness, acidity, tannins, weight, and intensity, you can start playing with subtler nuances.

In addition to the fruitiness mentioned above—especially plums, cherries, and dark berries like blackberries, boysenberries, and black currants—some of the subtle flavors that you might find in a Merlot include green pepper, baking spices, chocolate, cedar, and herbs. So it works to add those flavors, or foods that complement them, to your dishes.

other thoughts

Some foods that are considered classic pairings with Merlot are duck and other gamier poultry, lamb, pork loin, mushrooms, beef (especially roast beef and filet mignon), and blue, fruity, and nutty cheeses.

roasted pecans with olive oil and salt

The drop-dead simplicity of these nuts seems contrary to their can't-stop-eating-them taste. They're salty, rich, crunchy, and sweet all at the same time. Serve them as a snack at a party, a nibble before dinner, or an accompaniment to an afternoon glass of wine.

• MAKES 5 CUPS

5 cups raw pecans (about 1 pound)
2 tablespoons extra virgin olive oil
1½ teaspoons coarse kosher salt

▓ Preheat the oven to 375°F.

▓ Spread the pecans onto a rimmed baking sheet in a single layer and bake until browned and fragrant, about 12 minutes (during the last few minutes, watch them carefully—nuts can go from browned to burnt very quickly).

▓ While the nuts are still warm, transfer them to a large bowl and add the olive oil and salt, tossing to thoroughly and evenly coat. Set the baking sheet over a wire rack, return the nuts to the baking sheet, and let them cool completely. (You can prepare the pecans up to a week in advance, storing them at room temperature in an airtight container.)

FOOD & WINE TIP Nuts, like wines, can have lots of tannins—that brown, papery skin on many of them is the source—and so they hold up well to that dry-mouth, tannic quality in wine.

orange and olive tapenade

You'd be hard-pressed to find a recipe that's easier to make than tapenade. Just add your ingredients to a food processor and—buzz, buzz, buzz—it's done. This particular combination gets a delicious fruitiness by including half of an orange.

If you like, add a hunk of blue cheese to the platter with your tapenade and crackers. It, too, will go nicely with the wine. • MAKES
ABOUT 1¾ CUPS

1 cup drained pitted brine-cured niçoise or kalamata olives
1 cup drained pimento-stuffed Spanish olives (martini olives)
½ small orange, cut into 6 chunks (including the peel)
¼ cup extra virgin olive oil
1 teaspoon freshly ground black pepper, or more to taste
Whole wheat crackers, for serving

▓ In the bowl of a food processor, combine the olives, orange (including the peel), olive oil, and pepper and pulse to make a coarse puree, scraping down the bowl as necessary. (You can prepare the tapenade up to 2 days in advance, storing it covered in the refrigerator. Return to room temperature before serving.)

▓ Taste, ideally with your wine, and add more pepper if you like. Transfer the tapenade to a small bowl and serve with the crackers on the side.

merlot and cab: often a perfect pairing

Because the renowned wines of Bordeaux are generally Merlot and Cabernet Sauvignon blends, most wine books deal with the varietals together, or in succession. But because tannin levels are so key to successful pairings, this book arranges the red wine chapters from light tannins to heavy—which leaves Merlot toward the middle and Cabernet Sauvignon at the end.

white cheddar with wine-soaked cherries and herbs

This is an incredible—and an incredibly easy—dish, one that beautifully dresses up a familiar and easily accessible cheese. Serve it at a party or a picnic, or as an afternoon snack with your favorite bottle of Merlot.

The cherries need a couple of days to soak, though, so remember to prepare them in advance. • **SERVES 4**

⅓ cup Merlot, or other dry red wine
2 tablespoons extra virgin olive oil
1 tablespoon balsamic vinegar
1 teaspoon herbes de Provence (see page 125)
¼ teaspoon coarse kosher salt
⅔ cup dried Bing or other sweet (not tart) dried cherries, coarsely chopped
8 ounces medium-sharp white Cheddar cheese
Whole wheat crackers, for serving

▥ In a medium glass or stain-resistant plastic container, combine the wine, olive oil, vinegar, herbes de Provence, and salt, whisking to dissolve the salt. Add the cherries, cover, and refrigerate for at least 2 days, stirring occasionally. (You can refrigerate the cherry mixture for up to a week, stirring occasionally.)

▥ Place the cheese on a platter and let it and the cherry mixture come to room temperature. Spoon the cherry mixture over and around the cheese. Serve with the crackers on the side.

FOOD & WINE TIP To make this a great pairing for Pinot Noir, substitute Pinot Noir for Merlot, red wine vinegar for balsamic vinegar, and dried cranberries for dried cherries. Voilà!

thyme and garlic bread

Who doesn't love garlic bread? Here, the already fabulous treat becomes even more special with the addition of thyme. • SERVES 4 TO 6

2 tablespoons unsalted butter, room temperature
2 tablespoons extra virgin olive oil
2 cloves garlic, pressed through a garlic press or minced
1½ teaspoons chopped fresh thyme
¼ teaspoon coarse kosher salt
½ baguette

In a medium bowl, combine the butter, olive oil, garlic, thyme, and salt. Set aside. (You can prepare the garlic butter up to 3 days in advance, storing it covered in the refrigerator. Return to room temperature before proceeding.)

Preheat the broiler and arrange a rack about 6 inches from the heat.

Split the half baguette in half lengthwise, making 2 open-faced pieces. Cut each into 6 pieces. Spread some of the butter mixture on the cut side of each piece, dividing it evenly. Arrange the bread on a rimmed baking sheet, buttered side up, and broil until lightly toasted, 1½ to 2 minutes. Serve hot.

FOOD & WINE TIP The rich, buttery nature of this dish makes it a natural to pair with Chardonnay as well.

lamb, bacon, and barley soup

Perfect for a fall or winter day, this soup is absolutely easy to make and thoroughly satisfying. Add a big hunk of bread and a crunchy salad, and you've got a hearty, warming meal.

Since it features lamb, the soup's a natural to pair with Merlot. And since it simmers for a good while, even the most inexpensive stew meat becomes deliciously tender. • SERVES 6 TO 8

6 slices bacon, cut crosswise into ¼-inch strips
1 onion, cut into ¼-inch dice
1 pound lamb stew meat, cut into ½-inch dice
2 tablespoons all-purpose flour
2 teaspoons coarse kosher salt, or more to taste
1 teaspoon freshly ground black pepper, or more to taste
8 cups reduced-sodium beef broth
3 cups reduced-sodium chicken broth
½ cup pearl barley
1 tablespoon red wine vinegar, or more to taste

▨ In a medium stockpot over medium heat, cook the bacon, stirring occasionally, until crisp and golden, 6 to 8 minutes. Use a slotted spoon to transfer the bacon to a paper towel-lined plate.

▨ Increase the heat to medium-high. Add the onion to the pot with the bacon fat and cook, stirring occasionally, until the onion is soft, about 2 minutes. Add the lamb and cook, stirring occasionally, until the lamb and the onion are brown, about 3 minutes. Sprinkle in the flour, salt, and pepper and cook, stirring occasionally, for 1 minute. Add the broths and barley, scraping up any browned bits in the pot. Bring to a boil, reduce to a simmer, and cook until the lamb and barley are tender, about 45 minutes. Stir in the vinegar and about half of the bacon. (You can prepare the soup up to 3 days in advance. Cool it, then store it covered in the refrigerator. Gently reheat before proceeding.)

▨ Taste, ideally with your wine, and add more vinegar, salt, and/or pepper if you like. Serve hot, garnished with the remaining bacon.

FOOD & WINE TIP Try this experiment. Leave the vinegar out of the soup and taste the soup with the wine. Notice how the wine tastes just the tiniest bit sour? Now stir the vinegar into the soup, then taste the soup, and taste the wine again. Notice how the wine tastes fruitier? While the soup doesn't taste vinegary, that hint of acid helps soften both the acids and the tannins in the wine, bringing out the fruit and making an even more perfect match.

chicken sandwichettes with raisin jam and pickled onions

Many of my favorite easy meals start with supermarket rotisserie chicken. I absolutely love its roasty, rich flavors, and how well they're complemented by both sweet and savory side dishes.

These small sandwiches, which get bright acidity from the onions and dark sweet-and-sour fruit flavors from the jam, would be a perfect centerpiece for an afternoon picnic. • **MAKES 8 SANDWICHETTES**

½ small red onion, halved and thinly sliced
6 tablespoons red wine vinegar
1½ teaspoons coarse kosher salt, divided
1⅓ cups raisins
¼ cup sugar
⅔ cup Merlot, or other dry red wine
2 tablespoons balsamic vinegar
¼ teaspoon ground cloves
¼ teaspoon freshly ground black pepper
One 1½- to 2-pound store-bought rotisserie chicken
8 whole wheat dinner rolls, split horizontally

▓ In a small bowl, combine the onion, red wine vinegar, and 1 teaspoon of the salt, stirring to dissolve the salt. Let the mixture stand at room temperature for at least 2 hours, stirring occasionally. (You can cover and refrigerate the onion mixture for up to 3 days, stirring occasionally.)

▓ In the bowl of a food processor, combine the raisins and sugar and process to chop the raisins, scraping down the bowl as necessary. Transfer the mixture to a medium saucepan and add the Merlot, balsamic vinegar, cloves, pepper, and the remaining ½ teaspoon of salt. Bring to a boil over high heat, reduce to a simmer, and cook, stirring occasionally, until the liquid is syrupy, about 5 minutes. Remove from the heat and set aside to cool. (You can prepare the raisin jam up to 3 days in advance. Cool it, then store it covered in the refrigerator.)

▓ Shred the chicken into bite-sized pieces (discard the skin and bones). Drain the onion mixture.

▓ Arrange the bottom halves of the rolls on a work surface. Spread with the raisin jam, then top with the chicken and pickled onions, dividing all evenly. Add the top halves of the rolls, cut in half if you like, and serve.

pan-seared duck breasts with fig vinegar sauce

There's a *Seinfeld* episode in which Elaine has been fasting and is beginning to have delusions about the foods she's craving. She starts to rave about duck. "Mountains of duck," she moans, "and not fatty duck, either—juicy, tender breasts of duck!"

I can so relate to that craving. There's nothing like juicy, tender breasts of duck.

There is, however, a trick to making them, to getting rid of the fat, which is right below the skin. What you do is score the breasts, then sear them, skin side down, which renders out the fat. It's not hard to do—it's just a little duck-cooking secret that will merit deliciously crisped skin and, yep, juicy, tender meat.

This recipe serves eight to twelve as a small plate or as a sharing-sized portion of a main course, but it will also serve six as an entrée.

• SERVES 8 TO 12

1 tablespoon extra virgin olive oil
1 shallot, halved and thinly sliced
½ cup fig balsamic vinegar, homemade (recipe follows) or store-bought
1¾ teaspoons coarse kosher salt, divided
6 boneless, skin-on duck breasts (2½ to 3 pounds)
1 teaspoon freshly ground black pepper

■ In a small saucepan over medium-high heat, warm the olive oil. Add the shallot and cook, stirring occasionally, until tender and starting to brown, about 2 minutes. Stir in the vinegar (be careful—the mixture may splatter) and ¼ teaspoon of the salt. Increase the heat to high, bring to a boil, and cook until the mixture is reduced to 6 tablespoons, 3 to 4 minutes. Remove from the heat and set aside to cool. (You can prepare the fig vinegar sauce up to 2 days in advance, storing it covered in the refrigerator. Return to room temperature before serving.)

■ Trim any silver skin from the meaty side of the duck breasts. If the tender is still attached (a duck breast can have a tender just like a chicken breast), scrape the tendon out and pat the tender back in place. Trim the edges of the skin so there's no more than ¼ inch of overhang. Use a sharp knife to score the skin in a crosshatch pattern, with the cuts about ½ inch apart, being careful not to cut into the meat. Sprinkle both sides of the duck with the remaining 1½ teaspoons of salt and the pepper.

Heat two large skillets over medium-high heat. Add the duck, skin side down, and cook for about 6 minutes, until brown. As the fat is rendered from the duck and collects in the pan, spoon it off once or twice. Reduce the heat to medium and continue cooking until much of the fat is rendered and the skin is crisp and deeply golden brown, 2 to 4 minutes. Turn and cook until an internal thermometer reads 140°F for medium rare, 4 to 6 minutes. Transfer the duck to a cutting board and let it rest, loosely covered with foil, for 5 minutes.

Cut the duck on a diagonal into ½-inch slices. Transfer to a platter or to individual plates, dividing it evenly. Drizzle with the fig vinegar sauce, along with any accumulated juices, and serve.

homemade fig balsamic vinegar · *Makes about ¾ cup*

Fig balsamic vinegar is available at better supermarkets and specialty food stores. But you can make it inexpensively at home. Just remember to plan in advance, because it takes a couple of days for the figgy flavor to infuse into the vinegar. Besides using it in Pan-Seared Duck Breasts with Fig Vinegar Sauce, you can drizzle fig balsamic vinegar over other roasted meats and use it in salad dressing.

1 cup balsamic vinegar
8 dried Mission figs, stems trimmed, quartered
1 tablespoon honey

In a food processor, combine the vinegar and figs and process to finely chop the figs, scraping down the bowl as necessary. Transfer the mixture to a small saucepan and add the honey. Bring barely to a boil over medium heat. Transfer to a heatproof container, cover, and let stand at room temperature, stirring occasionally, for 2 days. Strain through a fine-mesh sieve, pressing the solids. Discard the solids. (You can keep the fig balsamic vinegar for about a week, storing it covered in the refrigerator.)

spiced balsamic mushroom mélange

This recipe is inspired by an Indian seasoning called garam masala. Like curry powder, it's a blend of spices. But garam masala is typically a warmer, sweeter blend, often including cardamom, coriander, cinnamon, cloves, and black pepper, to name a few. Sometimes you can find garam masala in supermarkets and often, in specialty stores. But here, we're making up our own blend with spices that you probably already have on hand.

My husband prefers this dish with a sprinkling of crumbled feta cheese on top, but I'm on the fence. Sometimes I like the creaminess that the cheese adds and sometimes I prefer the simplicity of just the spiced, roasted mushrooms. Do whichever you prefer—or experiment and try both. • **SERVES 4**

6 tablespoons extra virgin olive oil
2 tablespoons balsamic vinegar
1 teaspoon coarse kosher salt
½ teaspoon freshly ground black pepper
½ teaspoon ground cinnamon
½ teaspoon ground cloves
½ teaspoon ground cumin
¼ teaspoon ground allspice
¼ teaspoon ground cardamom
¼ teaspoon ground coriander
1 pound mixed meaty mushrooms, such as white, brown, cremini, baby portobello, or shiitake, larger ones cut in half, stems removed from shiitakes (about 8 cups)
3 tablespoons crumbled feta cheese (about 1 ounce), optional
½ teaspoon chopped fresh flat-leaf parsley

▓ Preheat the oven to 450°F.

▓ In a large bowl, combine the olive oil, vinegar, salt, pepper, cinnamon, cloves, cumin, allspice, cardamom, and coriander. Add the mushrooms, tossing to thoroughly and evenly coat. Transfer the mixture to a rimmed baking sheet and bake until browned and tender, about 15 minutes, tossing halfway through.

▓ Transfer the mushroom mixture to a gratin dish, other decorative serving dish, or individual plates and sprinkle with the cheese, if using, and parsley. Serve hot, with forks or toothpicks for spearing the mushrooms.

zinfandel

Zinfandel was long thought to be America's own wine grape. But for years, researchers and growers had noticed a similarity to Italy's Primitivo. In the late 1990s, serious study of Zinfandel's heritage began. A few years and several DNA tests later, it was proven that Zinfandel and Primitivo are indeed the same grape, one that actually hails from Croatia!

Still, Zinfandel makes a decidedly Wild West sort of wine, one that's big and bold, with bright acid, juicy and often jammy fruit, sometimes high alcohol levels, and even some spice. A classic pairing with Zin? All-American barbecue.

But Zinfandel also pairs beautifully with Italian foods, especially the tomato-based dishes of the south. It even works well with mildly spicy Mexican, Indian, and even Moroccan dishes, plus all kinds of braised, grilled, and salty cured meats.

Generally speaking, if it's rich and robust, it'll work with rootin' tootin' Zinfandel.

zinfandel by another name

• *Primitivo.* This is the name for the same grape in Italy.

pairing with zinfandel

Although there are, of course, nuances to Zinfandel, the most important factors in food and wine pairing aren't a wine's nuances, but its broad strokes. If you learn a wine's overall characteristics and combine that information with the General Pairing Tips (page 6), you'll have a near-perfect pairing every time.

Broad characteristics:
• dry (not sweet)
• medium to high in acidity, crispness, or brightness
• medium to high in tannins
• medium to heavy weight
• medium to strong intensity

Pairs well with dishes that are:
• not sweet
• medium to high in acidity, crispness, or brightness
• medium to high in richness/meatiness/heaviness, acidity, or slight bitterness

- medium to heavy weight
- medium to strong intensity

For example, pepperoni pizza, steak tacos, or barbecued pork ribs.

fine-tuning

With Zinfandel, we're getting into medium to high tannins. So it almost always helps to have some form of richness/meatiness/heaviness or slight bitterness in a recipe you pair with it—think beef and other fatty proteins, plus bitter elements like olives, citrus zest, bitter greens, and charring from grilling.

To balance both the tannins and the acidity, salt and acid in the food remain important. And while spicy Zinfandel can handle somewhat spicy food, too much heat in a recipe can combine with the sometimes high alcohol level of Zinfandel to create too much of a good thing.

other nuances

Once you have a pairing that's working on the basis of sweetness, acidity, tannins, weight, and intensity, you can start playing with subtler nuances.

Some of the subtle flavors that you might find in a Zinfandel include cherries, red berries (especially raspberries and cranberries), blackberries, plums, jam, pepper, baking spices (especially cloves), oak, and herbs. So it works to add those flavors, or foods that complement them, to your dishes.

other thoughts

Some foods that are considered classic pairings with Zinfandel are barbecue and barbecue sauce, steaks and chops, sausages, pizza, strong and aged cheeses, burgers, and grilled, stewed, or braised meats.

chunky caponata

Like ratatouille, caponata is a deliciously gloppy eggplant compote
that's served as a salad, side dish, or relish. But caponata differs
in that it has an almost sweet-and-sour quality, thanks to raisins,
capers, and a hit of vinegar in the mix.

If you have any leftover caponata, try draping it over a just-grilled
steak, chicken breast, pork chop, or lamb chop. All those dishes
would be equally yummy with your favorite Zin. • **MAKES ABOUT 4 CUPS**

½ cup extra virgin olive oil, divided
1 pound eggplant, cut into ½-inch dice (you should have about
   6 cups)
1 red onion, cut into ½-inch dice
3 bay leaves
2 teaspoons coarse kosher salt, or more to taste
½ teaspoon freshly ground black pepper, or more to taste
3 cloves garlic, thinly sliced
6 tablespoons red wine vinegar, or more to taste
⅓ cup golden raisins
⅓ cup drained oil-packed julienned sun-dried tomatoes
2 tablespoons pine nuts, toasted (see page 26)
2 tablespoons drained capers
1 teaspoon sugar, or more to taste
Stone-ground or table water crackers, for serving

▓ In a large skillet over medium heat, warm ¼ cup of the olive oil.
Add the eggplant and cook, stirring occasionally, until browned and
tender, about 6 minutes. Transfer the eggplant to a large bowl. (If the
skillet is browned on the bottom, that's okay. If it's blackened, give it a
quick rinse and dry.)

▓ Return the skillet to medium heat and warm the remaining ¼ cup
of olive oil. Add the onion, bay leaves, salt, and pepper and cook, stirring occasionally, until the onion is tender, about 3 minutes. Add the
garlic and cook, stirring occasionally, until fragrant and tender, 30 to
60 seconds. Transfer the onion mixture to the bowl with the eggplant.

▓ While the eggplant and onion are still warm, mix in the vinegar,
raisins, sun-dried tomatoes, pine nuts, capers, and sugar. (You can
prepare the caponata up to 3 days in advance. Cool it, then store it
covered in the refrigerator. Return to room temperature or reheat it
slightly before proceeding.)

▓ Taste the caponata, ideally with your wine, and add more vinegar,
sugar, salt, and/or pepper if you like. Serve the caponata warm or at
room temperature with the crackers on the side.

chimichurri provolone toasts

Kind of a parsley pesto, chimichurri is a spicy, vinegary, olive oil sauce that's most often served with grilled meat. But it's great for giving zip to a variety of dishes, like these melted cheese toasts.

This recipe makes about twice as much chimichurri as you'll need, but it's virtually impossible to make less because the amount would be too small for the food processor to puree. Serve the leftover chimichurri draped over grilled chicken or salmon. • SERVES 4 TO 6

¼ cup extra virgin olive oil
2 tablespoons red wine vinegar
15 sprigs fresh flat-leaf parsley
Leaves from 3 sprigs fresh oregano
3 cloves garlic
½ chipotle pepper from a can of chipotle peppers in adobo sauce
   (see note on page 149)
½ teaspoon coarse kosher salt
¼ teaspoon freshly ground black pepper
½ baguette
1 cup shredded provolone cheese (about 4 ounces)

In the bowl of a food processor, combine the olive oil, vinegar, parsley, oregano, garlic, chipotle pepper, salt, and pepper and process to form a pesto-like sauce, scraping down the bowl as necessary. Set the chimichurri aside. (You can prepare the chimichurri up to 2 days in advance, storing it covered in the refrigerator. Return to room temperature before serving.)

Preheat the oven to 400°F.

Split the half baguette in half lengthwise, making 2 open-faced pieces. Cut each into 6 pieces. Arrange the bread on a rimmed baking sheet and bake until lightly browned, about 10 minutes, turning halfway through.

Remove the bread from the oven (leave the oven on) and top the cut sides of the bread with the cheese, dividing it evenly. Bake until the cheese is warm and melted, 3 to 4 minutes.

Meanwhile, transfer about half of the chimichurri to a small serving bowl or to individual bowls. (You can refrigerate any remaining chimichurri, covered, for about a week.)

Serve the toasts warm with the chimichurri on the side for spooning on top.

marinated olives with citrus and garlic

It's no coincidence that many great wine bars offer bowls of marinated olives to munch on—salty, creamy, meaty, and slightly fruity without being sweet, marinated olives complement a host of wines.

This particular concoction is ideal for fruity but tannic Zinfandel, and you can throw it together in about ten minutes. Just remember to do it a few days before you plan to serve the olives, so that they have a chance to absorb the flavors of the marinade.

• MAKES ABOUT 4 CUPS

1 small orange
1 lemon
⅔ cup extra virgin olive oil
2 tablespoons coarsely chopped fresh rosemary
2 large cloves garlic, thinly sliced
½ teaspoon dried crushed red pepper flakes
4 cups drained assorted brine-cured olives (see below)

Use a vegetable peeler to cut the colored part of the peel from half of the orange and half of the lemon. Cut the peel into thin slices (save the remaining fruit for another use).

In a large bowl, combine the citrus peel, olive oil, rosemary, garlic, and red pepper. Add the olives, tossing to combine. Transfer the mixture to a container, cover, and refrigerate for at least 2 days, stirring occasionally. (You can refrigerate the olive mixture for up to 5 days, stirring occasionally.)

Let the olives come to room temperature before serving.

NOTE You probably won't find an assortment of olives all in one jar, but you can buy different kinds and combine them, or put together your own assortment if your supermarket has an olive bar.

FOOD & WINE TIP The bright yet rich nature of these olives also makes them a great match for Chardonnay.

bresaola-wrapped pecorino

Bresaola is a type of Italian dried meat, similar to prosciutto in that it's air-dried and typically enjoyed thinly sliced in an antipasto, but different in that it's made from beef. Increasingly, deli counters at better stores are carrying it. But if you can't find it, don't worry. The dish is absolutely just as good made with Italian dry salami.

For the cheese, you might notice several different types of pecorino at the store. Any type will work, but avoid one that's very hard and aged, like a good Parmesan might be, because it could be too brittle to cut into nice sticks. • SERVES 6 TO 8

8 ounces pecorino cheese
1 tablespoon balsamic vinegar
½ teaspoon coarse kosher salt
¼ teaspoon freshly ground black pepper
4 cups loosely packed arugula (about 2 ounces)
24 thin slices bresaola (about 5 ounces) (see above) or Italian
  dry salami (3 to 4 ounces)

▨ Cut the cheese into sticks, about ¼ x ¼ x 2½ inches (you should have about 24 sticks, with some odd-sized pieces left over). Set aside. (You can cut the cheese up to a day in advance, storing it covered in the refrigerator.)

▨ In a large bowl, combine the vinegar, salt, and pepper, whisking to dissolve the salt. Add the arugula, tossing to combine. Set aside.

▨ Arrange the bresaola slices on a work surface. Place 1 cheese stick and 3 to 4 arugula leaves across each slice, arranging the arugula so that the tops of the leaves stick out over one edge of the bresaola. Wrap each bresaola slice over the cheese and arugula (bresaola will often stick to itself—if it doesn't, moisten the seal with some liquid from the arugula mixture and/or secure it with a toothpick).

▨ Arrange the wrapped cheese on a platter or on individual plates and serve. (You can prepare the wrapped cheese up to an hour in advance, storing it covered in the refrigerator.)

black bean nachos with chipotle salsa and sour cream

I'd be the first one to argue that the ultimate beverage for a plate of ooey, gooey nachos is a margarita. Or a beer. But if you're in the mood for wine, Zinfandel works beautifully with nachos, especially this recipe, which gets a Zin-friendly kick from a chipotle pepper in the salsa. • SERVES 4

2 small tomatoes, diced (you should have 1 to 1¼ cups)
¼ red onion, finely diced
2 tablespoons chopped fresh cilantro, plus a sprig for garnish
1 chipotle pepper from a can of chipotle peppers in adobo sauce, minced (see below)
2 cloves garlic, pressed through a garlic press or minced
½ teaspoon coarse kosher salt
Half of a 13-ounce bag tortilla chips
One 15-ounce can black beans, drained
8 ounces shredded sharp Cheddar cheese (about 2 cups)
6 scallions, white and light green parts only, thinly sliced
½ cup sour cream

▓ In a medium bowl, combine the tomatoes, onion, chopped cilantro, chipotle pepper, garlic, and salt. (You can prepare the salsa up to 4 hours in advance, storing it covered in the refrigerator.)

▓ Preheat the oven to 450°F.

▓ On a large ovenproof platter or in a 2- to 3-quart shallow baking dish, arrange one-fourth of the chips. Top with one-fourth of the beans, one-fourth of the cheese, and one-fourth of the scallions. Repeat three times, making 4 layers. Bake the nachos until the cheese is melted, 6 to 8 minutes.

▓ Top the nachos with the salsa. Mound the sour cream in the middle, garnish with the cilantro sprig, and serve hot.

NOTE Canned chipotle peppers in adobo sauce are available in the ethnic or Latin section of most major supermarkets. Besides using them in this recipe, you can use them in Chimichurri Provolone Toasts (page 145), in other Latin dishes, and to give a smoky heat to your favorite stir-fries.

FOOD & WINE TIP The spicy yet creamy, cool nature of this dish makes it a natural for pairing with Rosé as well.

steak salad with tomatoes, parmesan, and dijon vinaigrette

You can definitely enjoy red wine with salad, especially if it's a hearty salad like this one, where although the portions are light, the flavors are bold. Ingredients that help make the bridge to Zinfandel include not only the grilled steak but also the bright vinaigrette, playing off the acid in the wine, and the slightly bitter radicchio, playing off the tannins. • **SERVES 6**

4 teaspoons red wine vinegar
2 cloves garlic, pressed through a garlic press or minced
1 teaspoon Dijon mustard
1 teaspoon coarse kosher salt, divided
½ teaspoon freshly ground black pepper, divided
3 tablespoons extra virgin olive oil
1 ounce Parmesan cheese
12 ounces boneless sirloin steak or flank steak, about ¾ inch thick
6 cups loosely packed mixed salad greens (about 3 ounces)
½ small red onion, halved and thinly sliced
½ head radicchio, halved, cored, and cut into ¼-inch shreds
  (you should have 2¾ to 3 cups)
9 cherry tomatoes, halved

▨ In a small bowl, combine the vinegar, garlic, mustard, ½ teaspoon of the salt, and ¼ teaspoon of the pepper, whisking to dissolve the salt. Whisk in the olive oil. Set aside. (You can prepare the dressing up to 3 days in advance, storing it covered in the refrigerator. Return to room temperature before serving.)

▨ Use a vegetable peeler to cut the cheese into thick shaves (you should have about ⅓ cup). Set aside. (You can shave the cheese up to a day in advance, storing it covered in the refrigerator.)

▨ Prepare the grill to high heat and lightly oil the grate. Sprinkle the steak with the remaining ½ teaspoon of salt and ¼ teaspoon of pepper. Grill to desired doneness, about 4 minutes per side for medium rare. Remove the steak from the grill and let it rest, loosely covered with foil, for 5 minutes.

▨ Meanwhile, in a large bowl, combine the greens, onion, and radicchio with about half of the dressing. Arrange the mixture on a platter or on individual plates, dividing it evenly.

▨ Cut the steak across the grain diagonally into thin slices. Arrange the steak and tomatoes over the greens. Drizzle with the remaining dressing, sprinkle with the cheese, and serve.

spice-rubbed chicken wings

I recently read that chicken wings have become the most popular appetizer in the United States, surpassing nachos. This simple recipe is a good example of why. Even though they're not cooked on the grill, these wings have a classic barbecue flavor. They're juicily, deliciously, finger-licking good! • SERVES 4 TO 6

2 tablespoons smoked paprika (see note on page 100)
2 tablespoons chili powder
4 teaspoons coarse kosher salt
4 teaspoons packed light brown sugar
1 tablespoon granulated garlic powder
1 tablespoon granulated onion powder
1½ teaspoons dried thyme
9 chicken wings (about 2 pounds)

In a shallow bowl, combine the paprika, chili powder, salt, brown sugar, garlic powder, onion powder, and thyme. (You can prepare the rub up to 2 weeks in advance, storing it in an airtight container at room temperature.)

Preheat the oven to 425°F. Lightly oil a rimmed baking sheet.

Use poultry shears or a sharp knife to cut off the wing tips (discard them or save them for another use), then halve the wings at the joint. Dredge the wing pieces in the rub and place the coated pieces on the prepared baking sheet.

Bake the wings until cooked through, 30 to 35 minutes, turning halfway through. Serve hot.

FOOD & WINE TIP While it's quite classic to combine Zinfandel and barbecue, or barbecue flavors, this recipe would also pair perfectly with Rosé.

meatballs with parmesan and spicy tomato sauce

If you're looking for a hearty hot appetizer, look no further than these tender, full-flavored meatballs—this dish is a guaranteed crowd-pleaser.

That said, I also like these as a first course for a dinner party. They're quite pretty in individual shallow bowls, four or five meatballs per serving, nestled in a pool of sauce. For a main course, serve them on a bed of pasta. • MAKES ABOUT 30 MEATBALLS WITH SAUCE

Two ¾-inch-thick slices French or Italian bread (about 2 ounces)
¼ cup whole, low-fat, or nonfat milk
1 large egg
2 cloves garlic, pressed through a garlic press or minced
1½ teaspoons coarse kosher salt
½ teaspoon freshly ground black pepper
⅔ cup plus 2 tablespoons grated Parmesan cheese (4 to 5 ounces), divided
3 tablespoons chopped fresh flat-leaf parsley, divided
1 pound 85 percent lean ground beef
4 ounces hot or spicy Italian sausage
2 tablespoons extra virgin olive oil
About 4 cups Spicy Tomato Sauce (recipe follows)

Remove the crusts from the bread, then tear the bread into rough 1-inch pieces. In a small bowl, combine the bread and the milk and set aside for 5 minutes.

Meanwhile, in a large bowl, whisk together the egg, garlic, salt, pepper, ⅔ cup of the cheese, and 2 tablespoons of the parsley.

Lightly squeeze the milk from the bread and shred the bread into the bowl with the egg mixture. Gently stir to combine. Add the beef and sausage and gently mix until well combined. With dampened hands, shape the mixture into about 30 meatballs, 1 to 1¼ inches in diameter. (You can shape the meatballs up to a day in advance, storing them covered in the refrigerator. Return to room temperature before proceeding.)

In a large skillet over medium heat, warm the olive oil. Without crowding the pan, add the meatballs and cook, turning occasionally, until lightly browned on all sides, 7 to 9 minutes (you may have to do this in batches). Transfer the browned meatballs to a plate and set aside.

(continued on next page)

In a medium stockpot over medium heat, bring the tomato sauce to a gentle boil. Reduce to a simmer and add the meatballs. Cook, gently stirring occasionally, until the meatballs are cooked through, about 10 minutes. Transfer the mixture to a casserole or chafing dish, or to individual plates, dividing it evenly, and sprinkle with the remaining 2 tablespoons of cheese and 1 tablespoon of parsley. Serve hot, with forks or toothpicks for spearing the meatballs.

spicy tomato sauce · *Makes about 4 cups*

I readily admit that when it comes to Italian cuisine, my husband is the better cook. This is basically his recipe, although it features a secret ingredient from my Jewish grandmother's version—a dash of hot sauce.

1 tablespoon extra virgin olive oil
½ onion, cut into ¼-inch dice
4 cloves garlic, pressed through a garlic press or minced
One 28-ounce can crushed tomatoes
¼ cup tomato paste (about half of a 6-ounce can)
¼ cup Zinfandel, or other dry red wine
1 tablespoon chopped fresh basil
1½ teaspoons chopped fresh oregano
½ teaspoon coarse kosher salt
½ teaspoon hot sauce, such as Tabasco
1½ teaspoons sugar, optional

In a large saucepan or small stockpot over medium heat, warm the olive oil. Add the onion and cook, stirring occasionally, until tender, 4 to 6 minutes (adjust the heat, if necessary, to avoid browning). Add the garlic and cook, stirring occasionally, until fragrant, about 30 seconds. Stir in the tomatoes (with their juices) and tomato paste, increase the heat to high, and bring to a boil. Remove from the heat and stir in the wine, basil, oregano, salt, and hot sauce. Taste, ideally with your wine, and if the sauce is too acidic or makes the wine seem tasteless or watery, stir in the sugar. (You can prepare the sauce in advance, storing it covered in the refrigerator for up to a week or in the freezer for several months. Thaw in the refrigerator before reheating.)

FOOD & WINE TIP Although it's not a wine covered in this book, Chianti, made from the Sangiovese grape, would also be a great match with this dish.

syrah

One of the incredible things about working on this book has been spending quality time with each varietal as I developed the recipes to go with it. For many of the wines, I got to know them on a much deeper level and came away with new awe and appreciation for them—much as you might after spending a concentrated period of time with a good friend.

Syrah is one for which that's particularly true. While I always liked it fine before, I've come to absolutely love it.

Syrah is kind of a low-down-and-dirty wine—and I mean that in a good way. You often hear it described as meaty, and although that sounds strange for a wine, it's very true. Syrah is also earthy and inky and funky and fruity. It's kind of like a great blues bar or a perfectly worn-in pair of jeans. You might not want to wear worn-in jeans, or drink Syrah, all the time. But when they fit, they fit like nothing else.

syrah by another name

• *Shiraz.* This is the name for the same grape in Australia. • *Rhône wines.* As with other French wines, these French Syrahs are labeled with the name of the area they're from. They might have the general area name Rhône Valley, or names of subregions within the Rhône (Côte-Rôtie, for example). Basically, any red wine from the northern Rhône will be 100 percent Syrah, while any red wine from the southern Rhône will be a blend of mostly Syrah and Grenache.

pairing with syrah

Although there are, of course, nuances to Syrah, the most important factors in food and wine pairing aren't a wine's nuances, but its broad strokes. If you learn a wine's overall characteristics and combine that information with the General Pairing Tips (page 6), you'll have a near-perfect pairing every time.

Broad characteristics:
• dry (not sweet)
• medium to high in acidity, crispness, or brightness
• medium to high in tannins
• heavy weight
• strong intensity

Pairs well with dishes that are:

- not sweet
- medium to high in acidity, crispness, or brightness
- medium to high in richness/meatiness/heaviness, acidity, or slight bitterness
- heavy weight
- strong intensity

For example, marinated grilled steak, wine-braised short ribs, or garlic-rosemary leg of lamb.

fine-tuning

Even more tannins in Syrah, plus the wine's uniquely meaty flavors, mean that even more meatiness in the food will help your pairings. The kinds of meats that seem to work best with Syrah are ones that are similarly earthy—grilled meats, cured meats, spicy meats. You can also use other "meaty" ingredients—like sun-dried tomatoes, olives, and cheese.

Of course, salt and acid remain important. As with Merlot, which has similar dark fruit flavors to Syrah, balsamic vinegar is a great tool.

other nuances

Once you have a pairing that's working on the basis of sweetness, acidity, tannins, weight, and intensity, you can start playing with subtler nuances.

In addition to the meatiness mentioned above, some of the subtle flavors that you might find in a Syrah include dark berries (especially blackberries, boysenberries, and black currants), black cherries, black olives, bacon, pepper, baking spices (especially cloves), smoke, cocoa, and herbs. So it works to add those flavors, or foods that complement them, to your dishes.

other thoughts

Some foods that are considered classic pairings with Syrah are beef, lamb, barbecue and barbecue sauce, grilled foods, braised dishes and stews, sausages, mushrooms, aged and hard cheeses, and tuna steak.

jack cheese with tomato-lemon compote

Cheese and crackers really is the ultimate nibble for a glass of wine. But sometimes you want to dress it up a bit, put a little more effort into it. For those times, I often like to make a jam, compote, or spread that will complement both the cheese and the wine. This one is especially designed for Syrah, with fresh tomatoes and lemon providing bright acidity and sun-dried tomatoes providing a low, savory quality. And it's easy to make, taking less than 10 minutes of hands-on time. • SERVES 4

1 lemon
1½ cups halved cherry tomatoes, ideally a mix of colors
¼ cup drained oil-packed julienned sun-dried tomatoes
¼ cup Syrah, or other dry red wine
1 teaspoon chopped fresh thyme
½ teaspoon coarse kosher salt
½ teaspoon freshly ground black pepper
8 ounces Monterey Jack cheese
Stone-ground crackers, for serving

▒ Use a vegetable peeler to cut the colored part of the peel from the lemon. Cut the peel into thin slices. Halve the lemon and squeeze 1 tablespoon of juice (save the remaining lemon for another use).

▒ In a medium saucepan over medium heat, combine the sliced lemon peel, lemon juice, cherry tomatoes, sun-dried tomatoes, wine, thyme, salt, and pepper and bring to a boil. Reduce to a simmer and cook, stirring occasionally, until the mixture resembles a chunky jam, about 20 minutes. Set aside to cool slightly. (You can prepare the compote up to 2 days ahead. Cool it, then store it covered in the refrigerator. Gently reheat before serving.)

▒ Place the cheese on a platter and let it to come to room temperature. Serve the compote and crackers on the side.

FOOD & WINE TIP This compote is also incredible draped over roasted fish, a dish that would pair well with Syrah.

chunky beef and syrah chili

Here's a hearty, full-flavored chili, brimming with big chunks of beef. Topped with mild salsa and sour cream, it has a Latin slant—try it with warm corn tortillas on the side.

The recipe makes enough for a first-course serving for six. If you want to make it an entrée for six, simply double the ingredients (and use a very large pot). • **SERVES 6**

2 cups dried red kidney beans (about 1 pound)
2 tablespoons extra virgin olive oil
2 onions (about 1 pound), cut into ½-inch dice
1 pound beef stew meat, cut into ¾-inch dice
4 cloves garlic, pressed through a garlic press or minced
1 tablespoon chili powder
1 tablespoon coarse kosher salt, or more to taste
2 teaspoons dried oregano
2 teaspoons dried sage
1 teaspoon ground coriander
1 teaspoon ground cumin
1 teaspoon freshly ground black pepper, or more to taste
1 cup Syrah, or other dry red wine
One 14-ounce can diced fire-roasted tomatoes
2 teaspoons soy sauce
¾ cup mild tomato salsa, homemade or store-bought
6 tablespoons sour cream

▦ Place the beans in a large pot, bowl, or other container and cover with water by at least 4 inches. Set aside in the refrigerator overnight. The next day, drain the beans and set aside.

▦ In a large stockpot over medium-high heat, warm the olive oil. Add the onions and cook, stirring occasionally, for 2 minutes. Add the beef and cook, stirring occasionally, until the beef and onions are brown, 6 to 8 minutes. Add the garlic, chili powder, salt, oregano, sage, coriander, cumin, and pepper and cook, stirring occasionally, for 1 minute. Stir in the wine, scraping up any browned bits in the bottom of the pot. Stir in the beans, tomatoes (with their juices), and 4 cups of water. Bring to a boil, reduce to a simmer, and cook, stirring occasionally, until the beans and meat are tender, about 1½ hours. Remove from the heat and stir in the soy sauce. (You can prepare the chili up to 3 days in advance. Cool it, then store it covered in the refrigerator. Reheat before proceeding.)

▦ Taste the chili, ideally with your wine, and add more salt and/or pepper if you like. Serve hot, garnished with the salsa and sour cream.

bacon-wrapped halibut bites with balsamic drizzle

These amazing little morsels are light and delicate, thanks to the fish. They're smoky and savory, thanks to the bacon. And they're ever so slightly sweet, thanks to a syrupy balsamic sauce. • SERVES 4 TO 6

¼ cup balsamic vinegar
1 teaspoon Dijon mustard
12 slices bacon, halved crosswise
1 pound skinless halibut fillets, cut into 1-inch cubes (you should have about 24 pieces)
½ teaspoon freshly ground black pepper
¼ teaspoon coarse kosher salt

▓ In a small saucepan over high heat, bring the vinegar to a boil and cook until it's reduced to 2 tablespoons, 2 to 3 minutes. Remove from the heat and whisk in the mustard. Set aside to cool. (You can prepare the balsamic drizzle up to a day in advance, storing it covered in the refrigerator. Return to room temperature before serving.)

▓ Wrap a piece of bacon around each piece of fish, securing it with a wooden toothpick. (You can prepare the bacon-wrapped fish up to 4 hours in advance, storing it covered in the refrigerator. Return to room temperature before proceeding.)

▓ Preheat the oven to 450°F. Lightly coat a rimmed baking sheet with safflower, sunflower, peanut, or other high-heat cooking oil and preheat the baking sheet.

▓ Once the baking sheet is hot, remove it from the oven and quickly arrange the bacon-wrapped fish on it so that an exposed side of the fish faces up. Bake for 10 minutes. Carefully turn the bacon-wrapped fish over and bake until the bacon is lightly browned and the fish is cooked through, about 5 minutes. Set the fish aside to cool slightly.

▓ Meanwhile, drizzle the balsamic drizzle decoratively onto a platter or onto individual plates.

▓ Arrange the bacon-wrapped fish on top of the balsamic drizzle, sprinkle with the salt and pepper, and serve hot.

FOOD & WINE TIP While the delicate taste of the halibut provides a nice counterpoint to the richness of the bacon, the fish isn't adding any flavors that are particularly key to the pairing. So if you like, you can substitute another firm, white-fleshed fish, or even boneless, skinless chicken.

peppercorn-crusted tuna

Just like salmon and Pinot Noir, tuna and Syrah is considered a classic fish and red wine pairing. It works because tuna has a distinct meatiness to it, making it heavy enough for the wine. • **SERVES 6**

¾ cup Syrah, or other dry red wine
2 teaspoons soy sauce
1 clove garlic, pressed through a garlic press or minced
1 tablespoon unsalted butter
2 tablespoons green peppercorns (dried, not packed in brine) (see below)
1½ teaspoons coarse kosher salt
1 pound raw tuna steaks, about 1½ inches thick
2 tablespoons safflower, sunflower, peanut, or other high-heat cooking oil
3 cups loosely packed arugula (about 1½ ounces)
½ small head radicchio, cored and cut into ¼-inch shreds (you should have about 2 cups)

▓ In a small saucepan over high heat, combine the wine, soy sauce, and garlic and bring to a boil. Reduce to a simmer and cook, stirring occasionally, for 5 minutes. Remove from the heat and stir in the butter. Set aside to cool. (You can prepare the sauce up to a day in advance, storing it covered in the refrigerator. Reheat slightly before serving.)

▓ Meanwhile, use a mortar and pestle to lightly crush the peppercorns. (If you don't have a mortar and pestle, place them in a small bowl and lightly crush them with the end of a wooden spoon.) Stir in the salt. Press the peppercorn mixture evenly over one side of the tuna.

▓ In a medium skillet over medium-high heat, warm the oil. Add the tuna, crusted side down, and cook until well seared, about 3 minutes per side for medium rare. Transfer the tuna to a cutting board and let it rest, loosely covered with foil, for 5 minutes.

▓ Meanwhile, in a medium bowl, combine the arugula and radicchio. Arrange the mixture on a platter or on individual plates, dividing it evenly.

▓ Cut the tuna into ½-inch slices and arrange it on top of the arugula mixture. Serve the wine sauce on the side for dipping.

> **NOTE** Dried green peppercorns are available in the spice section at better supermarkets. Besides using them in this recipe, you can crush them and press them into steaks and chops, stir them into mayonnaise and aïoli, and sprinkle them over salads.

wine-soused sausages, onions, and peppers with mint

A wine-y version of one of my favorite combinations, the sausage-onion-pepper trio is served with a mint garnish that nicely complements the herbaceous notes in the wine.

If you want to turn the dish into an entrée, serve it over polenta or rice, or as a hero sandwich, piled onto a warm, soft roll. • SERVES 6

2 tablespoons extra virgin olive oil
2 red bell peppers, cored, seeded, and cut into ¼-inch slices
1 onion, quartered and cut into ¼-inch slices
1½ teaspoons coarse kosher salt
1½ teaspoons freshly ground black pepper
12 ounces precooked chicken sun-dried tomato or chicken
   portobello mushroom sausages, cut diagonally into ½-inch slices
1 cup Syrah, or other dry red wine
2 tablespoons thinly sliced fresh mint leaves

▨ In a large skillet over medium-high heat, warm the olive oil. Add the red peppers and cook, stirring occasionally, for 2 minutes. Add the onion, salt, and pepper and cook, stirring occasionally, until the red peppers and onion are starting to soften, about 2 minutes. Reduce the heat to low and cook, stirring occasionally, until the red peppers and onion are very soft, 10 to 12 minutes. Transfer the mixture to a plate and set aside.

▨ Return the skillet to medium-high heat and add the sausages. Cook, stirring occasionally, until the sausages are nicely browned, 3 to 4 minutes. Add the wine, stirring up any browned bits on the bottom of the skillet, and bring to a boil. Cook, stirring occasionally, until the wine is almost entirely evaporated, 2 to 3 minutes. Return the red pepper and onion mixture to the skillet, stirring until heated through. Transfer the mixture to a casserole or chafing dish, or to individual plates, dividing it evenly. Sprinkle with the mint and serve.

FOOD & WINE TIP If you want a wine to work *with* a recipe, it always helps to put the wine *in* the recipe.

pizza with salami, mozzarella, and fresh herbs

Italian dry salami has a beautiful affinity to Syrah. Both are meaty, rich, peppery, and the slightest bit herbal. It's a match made in heaven.

Here, the flavors of the salami are complemented by rosemary and basil. Softly sweet and creamy, fresh mozzarella adds a nice counterpoint. • SERVES 4 TO 8

One 12-ounce pizza dough, homemade or store-bought
1 tablespoon extra virgin olive oil
¼ cup shredded Asiago cheese (about 1 ounce)
1 tablespoon chopped fresh rosemary
16 to 18 thin slices Italian dry salami (2 to 3 ounces)
4 ounces fresh mozzarella cheese, cut into ¼-inch slices
2 tablespoons chopped fresh basil, or 12 to 16 whole fresh basil leaves

▤ Preheat the oven, along with a pizza stone if you have one, to 500°F.

▤ On a lightly floured work surface, roll or stretch the dough out to a 12- to 14-inch round. Transfer the dough to a pizza pan or a flour- or cornmeal-dusted pizza paddle. Brush with the olive oil and sprinkle with the Asiago cheese and rosemary. Top with the salami and mozzarella cheese. Transfer the pizza to the oven and bake for 10 to 12 minutes, until the pizza is golden and crisp.

▤ Sprinkle the pizza with the basil, cut into wedges, and serve.

FOOD & WINE TIP The big tannins of Syrah are complemented by nuts that are also high in tannins, like walnuts. Try a few sprinkled on top of the pizza with the basil. It's a little kooky—but it's good!

grilled rosemary steak skewers with parmesan sauce

I have to admit that it somewhat pains me to take a beautiful steak and cut it up for skewers. That pain, however, is more than worth the pleasure of these carnivorously satisfying ribbons. The combination of the flavorful grilled meat, earthy rosemary, and salty, savory Parmesan—washed down with a sip of Syrah—is divine. • SERVES 6

½ cup grated Parmesan cheese (2½ to 3 ounces)
½ cup sour cream
2 tablespoons whipping cream
1 tablespoon fresh lemon juice
1 teaspoon prepared horseradish
1¼ teaspoons coarse kosher salt, divided
1¼ teaspoons freshly ground black pepper, divided
1½ pounds rib-eye or New York steaks, trimmed and cut
    diagonally into ½-inch strips (you should have about 18 pieces)
3 tablespoons extra virgin olive oil
1 tablespoon chopped fresh rosemary
Special equipment: about eighteen 8-inch skewers, soaked in
    water for at least 10 minutes if they're wood or bamboo

▓ In a small bowl, combine the cheese, sour cream, cream, lemon juice, horseradish, ¼ teaspoon of the salt, and ¾ teaspoon of the pepper. Set aside. (You can prepare the Parmesan sauce up to 2 days in advance, storing it covered in the refrigerator. Return to room temperature before serving.)

▓ Thread the steak onto skewers, one strip per skewer. Brush both sides with the olive oil and sprinkle with the rosemary, the remaining 1 teaspoon of salt, and the remaining ½ teaspoon of pepper.

▓ Prepare the grill to medium-high heat. Grill the skewers to desired doneness, about 2½ minutes per side for medium. Remove the steak from the grill and let it rest, loosely covered with foil, for 5 minutes.

▓ Serve the steak skewers with the Parmesan sauce on the side.

cabernet sauvignon

C abernet Sauvignon is undoubtedly the planet's most popular and respected grape.

In fact, we have Cabernet Sauvignon to thank for the great wines of Bordeaux's Left Bank, possibly the best there are. We have Cabernet Sauvignon to thank for the acclaimed wines of California and many of us have Cabernet to thank for first seducing us into the world of wine.

One of the qualities that many love about Cabernet is a certain austerity, a kind of sharp, severity in the wine that comes from typically big, bold tannins.

For food and wine pairing, however, that quality can be limiting. In other words, you have to narrow your aim a bit with Cab. But when you hit the target, a Cabernet pairing is that much more exciting, inspiring, and satisfying.

cabernet sauvignon by another name

• *Bordeaux, Red Bordeaux.* As with other French wines, these French Cabernet Sauvignon blends are labeled with the name of the area they're from. They might have the general name Bordeaux, or the names of subregions within Bordeaux (Médoc, for example). In blends from the Left Bank of Bordeaux, Cabernet will be the dominant grape. On the Right Bank, Cabernet Sauvignon will likely be part of the blend, but a minor player. • *Meritage.* A group of American vintners have trademarked this name, pronounced to rhyme with "heritage," for Bordeaux-style blends made in the United States. These wines often include Cabernet Sauvignon but may or may not be mostly Cab.

pairing with cabernet sauvignon

Although there are, of course, nuances to Cabernet Sauvignon, the most important factors in food and wine pairing aren't a wine's nuances, but its broad strokes. If you learn a wine's overall characteristics and combine that information with the General Pairing Tips (page 6), you'll have a near-perfect pairing every time.

Broad characteristics:
• dry (not sweet)
• medium to high in acidity, crispness, or brightness
• high in tannins

- heavy weight
- strong intensity

Pairs well with dishes that are:
- not sweet
- medium to high in acidity, crispness, or brightness
- high in richness/meatiness/heaviness, acidity, or slight bitterness
- heavy weight
- strong intensity

For example, prime rib, steak with blue cheese, or grilled lamb chops.
The biggest consideration, though, are the tannins. Make sure your dishes have enough meatiness, acidity, bitterness, and/or salt to work with Cabernet Sauvignon.

fine-tuning

Although there aren't a wide variety of foods that go with Cabernet Sauvignon, as long as you're using one or more of them, your pairings should sing.

Playing with salt and acid levels will help marry a dish to your particular bottle of Cab, as will adding rich/meaty/heavy and/or bitter elements. Ways to add bitterness to a dish include charring an ingredient, adding bitter greens like endive or radicchio, and adding walnuts or pecans.

other nuances

Once you have a pairing that's working on the basis of sweetness, acidity, tannins, weight, and intensity, you can start playing with subtler nuances.

Some of the subtle flavors that you might find in a Cabernet Sauvignon include dark berries (especially blackberries, boysenberries, and black currants), black cherries, green pepper, baking spices (especially cloves), cedar, tobacco, and eucalyptus. So it works to add those flavors, or foods that complement them, to your dishes.

other thoughts

Some foods that are considered classic pairings with Cabernet Sauvignon are beef in almost any form (especially steak and prime rib), lamb, venison, grilled foods, and aged, blue, and sometimes stinky cheeses.

rosemary walnuts

If you've got five minutes, you can make this recipe. But don't mistake its simplicity for simplicity of flavor. These walnuts are a little sweet, a little sour, a little herbal, a little salty, and even a little meaty. Perfect for a glass of big, bold Cab.

They're delicious eaten out of hand, but if you're serving a Cabernet-friendly entrée and want a side dish that will also complement the wine, you can sprinkle them on top of a brown rice pilaf or other earthy grain dish, and the nuts will pull it all together. • **MAKES 2 CUPS**

    2 cups raw walnut halves (about 7 ounces)
    2 tablespoons balsamic vinegar
    1 teaspoon red wine vinegar
    2 teaspoons chopped fresh rosemary
    1 teaspoon coarse kosher salt

Heat a large nonstick skillet over medium heat. Add the walnuts and cook, stirring occasionally, until they're fragrant and toasted, 4 to 5 minutes. Remove the skillet from the heat and add the vinegars, rosemary, and salt, stirring until the mixture is evenly distributed and has been absorbed into the walnuts. Transfer the walnuts to a plate or platter to cool thoroughly before serving. (You can prepare the walnuts up to 4 hours in advance, storing them in an airtight container at room temperature.)

FOOD & WINE TIP Walnuts are about the most tannic nuts there are—that papery brown coating they have, folded into all those nooks and crannies, gives you the same dry-mouth feeling that you get from a strong red wine like Cabernet Sauvignon. And while it seems counter to logic, pairing tannic foods with tannic wines will actually decrease your overall sensation of tannins, allowing the rich, ripe fruit flavors in the wine to shine through.

focaccia with coffee-pepper dipping oil

You know how when you go to a nice, often Italian restaurant, they pour a little something into a shallow bowl for you to dip your bread into? This recipe is an enhanced version of one of those dipping sauces, the slight bitterness of the coffee making it especially perfect for Cabernet Sauvignon.

And while it's not imperative that you bake homemade focaccia to go with the sauce—you can buy focaccia in the bakery department at many major supermarkets these days—it's quite easy to make. There's nothing like fresh bread, still warm from the oven, and a glass of wine to celebrate it. • SERVES 4 TO 6

½ cup extra virgin olive oil
2 teaspoons coarsely ground unflavored coffee beans (see below)
2 teaspoons coarsely ground black pepper
1 tablespoon soy sauce
1 teaspoon Dijon mustard
Half of a 9 x 12-inch loaf focaccia bread, homemade (recipe follows) or store-bought, for serving

▓ In a small saucepan over medium heat, combine the olive oil, coffee, and pepper. When the mixture is almost at a simmer, remove the saucepan from the heat. Set aside to steep for 10 minutes.

▓ Whisk in the soy sauce and mustard. (You can prepare the dipping sauce up to 2 days in advance, storing it covered in the refrigerator. Return to room temperature before serving.)

▓ Cut the focaccia into about 1 x 4½-inch strips. Serve the dipping sauce in shallow bowls on the side.

> **NOTE** If you don't keep coarsely ground coffee beans on hand—or whole beans and a coffee grinder—just buy a tiny amount of whole beans, then use a mortar and pestle or the end of a wooden spoon to crush them to a coarse grind.

homemade focaccia bread

Makes one 9 x 12-inch loaf (about 1½ pounds)

This is the wildly popular focaccia I used to serve at the café I owned in Sausalito, just across the Golden Gate Bridge from San Francisco. The recipe doesn't need a lot of hands-on time, but it does need to be started at least a day before you plan to bake it.

2 teaspoons active dry yeast, divided
2¾ plus ⅔ cups all-purpose flour, divided
½ cup extra virgin olive oil, divided, plus more for the bowl and
   baking sheet
2 tablespoons plus ½ teaspoon coarse kosher salt, divided

Place ½ cup of warm water (118°F to 120°F) in a medium bowl. Sprinkle 1 teaspoon of the yeast on top of the water and set aside for 15 minutes (the mixture might not get foamy).

Stir in ⅔ cup of the flour. Loosely cover the bowl with plastic wrap and set aside at room temperature for 45 minutes.

Place 2 tablespoons of warm water (118°F to 120°F) in the bowl of an electric mixer that has a dough hook attachment. Sprinkle the remaining teaspoon of yeast on top of the water and set aside for 15 minutes (the mixture might not get foamy).

Add the flour mixture, 3 tablespoons of the olive oil, 2 tablespoons of the salt, and ⅔ cup of cool water to the mixer bowl, and stir lightly. Add the remaining 2¾ cup flour and use a dough hook to mix on medium-low speed for 2 minutes. Let the dough rest for 5 minutes, then mix again on medium-low for 4 minutes. The dough should be smooth and slightly sticky.

Place the dough in a lightly oiled bowl, rolling it to coat. Cover the bowl with plastic wrap, let it sit at room temperature for 30 minutes, then refrigerate it overnight. (You can prepare the dough in advance, storing it covered in the refrigerator for up to 2 days or in the freezer for several months. Thaw in the refrigerator before proceeding.)

Coat a rimmed baking sheet with olive oil. Place the dough on the baking sheet and gently coax it into about an 8 x 10-inch rectangle. Lightly cover the dough with plastic wrap and set it aside at room temperature until it expands to about 9 x 12 inches and is about 1½ inches tall, about 2 hours. Preheat the oven to 400°F.

Uncover the dough and use your fingertips to deeply dimple it. Drizzle the dough with the remaining 1 tablespoon of olive oil, then sprinkle it with the remaining ½ teaspoon of salt. Bake the focaccia until nicely browned, 25 to 30 minutes.

Transfer the baking pan with the focaccia to a wire rack to cool for 10 minutes. Remove the focaccia from the baking pan and return it to the wire rack to cool completely. (You can prepare the focaccia in advance, storing it covered in the freezer for up to a month. Thaw at room temperature before serving.)

charred eggplant spread with whole wheat pita toasts

If you like baba ghanoush—the popular Middle Eastern dip/ spread—you'll love this dish. Both feature creamy eggplant mixed with olive oil, lemon juice, and garlic. But while baba ghanoush includes tahini (a paste made from ground sesame seeds), this recipe adds a red bell pepper, along with bold grill-roasted flavors.

Serve it as a first course, as a snack, or as part of a Mediterranean-inspired meze plate. • **SERVES 6 TO 8**

1 globe eggplant (about 1 pound)
1 red bell pepper
2 teaspoons fresh lemon juice, or more to taste
2 cloves garlic
2 teaspoons coarse kosher salt, or more to taste
1 teaspoon freshly ground black pepper, or more to taste
½ cup extra virgin olive oil, divided
3 rounds whole wheat pita bread
1 teaspoon chopped fresh flat-leaf parsley

▨ Prepare the grill to medium-high heat. Place the eggplant and red pepper on the grill and cook, turning occasionally, until both are well charred on the outside and the eggplant is soft in the middle, 12 to 18 minutes. (You can also char the eggplant and pepper directly over a medium flame on a gas stovetop. Sit them each right on the grate over a burner, and cook, turning occasionally, until charred all over, 8 to 12 minutes.) Set aside until cool enough to handle.

▨ Peel the charred skin from the eggplant, leaving behind as much flesh as possible (it's okay if you don't get all of the skin off). Place the flesh in the bowl of a food processor.

▨ Use your fingers to wipe most of the charred skin from the red pepper, then cut or tear the red pepper in half and discard the core and seeds. Add the remaining red pepper to the food processor, along with the lemon juice, garlic, salt, pepper, and ¼ cup of the olive oil. Process to form a smooth puree, scraping down the bowl as necessary. Set aside. (You can prepare the eggplant spread up to 2 days in advance, storing it covered in the refrigerator. Return to room temperature before proceeding.)

▨ Preheat the oven to 375°F.

⬜ Cut the pitas in half. Split each half into two semicircles, then cut each semicircle into 4 wedges. Arrange the pita wedges on two baking sheets, smooth side down, and brush with 3 tablespoons of the remaining olive oil. Bake until lightly toasted, 10 to 12 minutes. Set aside to cool.

⬜ Taste the eggplant spread, ideally with your wine, and add more lemon juice, salt, and/or pepper if you like. Transfer the spread to a platter or shallow bowl, or to individual plates, dividing it evenly. Drizzle with the remaining 1 tablespoon of olive oil and garnish with the parsley. Serve the pita toasts on the side.

FOOD & WINE TIP Charring the eggplant and red pepper adds slightly bitter notes, which offset the tannins in the wine.

oh tannin bomb!

For some time now, one of the trends has been to make wines bigger and bigger and bolder and bolder, with more and more fruit and more and more intense tannins—as if the more explosive the sensation in your mouth, the better the wine.

Some chalk it up to the fact that critics sometimes taste so many wines at a time that it takes something really powerful to get their attention. I think it also has to do with an overall intensity craze—we're intrigued by darker and darker coffee, hotter and hotter salsa, bitterer and bitterer chocolate. But, um, does it taste good?

Sometimes boldness is pleasant. Sometimes subtlety is also pleasant. For that in a red wine, try a softer varietal, like Merlot. Or look for wines made with a lighter touch, or that have aged a little bit.

Mostly, that's what the tannins are there for—to give a wine ageability. After a few years, the tannins (and acids) will mellow and a former tannin bomb can become a soft, supple, beautifully delicious thing.

coppa-wrapped dates with blue cheese

This is a killer dish for a finger-foods kind of party—because although it's incredibly simple, it's also incredibly tasty, with complex sweet, savory, and salty flavors happening all at once. It's also one of those rare hot appetizers that you can prepare in advance and then, when you're ready, just pop it into the oven. Ten minutes later—mouth-wateringly delicious, warm morsels for your guests to enjoy.

You might be familiar with a version that was popular a few years ago, with bacon wrapped around the dates. While that's also great, the meatier, more beefy quality of coppa—although it's made from pork—better marries with the big flavors of Cabernet.

Coppa, sometimes called capicola, is increasingly available at the deli counters of better stores. But if you can't find it, don't stress about it. Simply use Italian dry salami.

For the dates, small is preferable, to keep the dish from being too sweet. So avoid big, plump Medjool dates and buy garden-variety packaged whole pitted dates. • SERVES 4 TO 6

24 pitted dates, preferably not Medjool (see above)
About ½ cup crumbled blue cheese (about 2 ounces)
24 thin slices coppa (sometimes called capicola) (see above) or
   Italian dry salami (3 to 4 ounces)

If there isn't one already, cut a lengthwise slit in each date. Fill each date with a generous ½ teaspoon of the cheese. Fold a piece of the coppa in half lengthwise, then wrap it around the date, securing it with a wooden toothpick (if the coppa doesn't fit around the date, just make a U shape, securing both ends with the toothpick). Arrange the wrapped dates, seam side up, on a rimmed baking sheet. (You can prepare the coppa-wrapped dates up to 4 hours in advance, storing them covered in the refrigerator. Return to room temperature before proceeding.)

Preheat the oven to 450°F.

Bake the dates until the coppa is slightly crisped and the cheese is bubbly, 7 to 9 minutes. Set aside to cool slightly before serving warm.

FOOD & WINE TIP This dish also works with Syrah.

camembert and black olive phyllo cigars

These little cigars will delicately shatter in your mouth, with thin layers of crisp phyllo giving way to a deliciously savory filling that beautifully complements the wine.

They're decidedly elegant, making them appropriate for any special occasion. And since they freeze well, you can keep them on hand and pop them into the oven whenever you're feeling festive.

• MAKES ABOUT 32

8 ounces Camembert cheese, cut into rough ¾-inch dice
1⅓ cups drained pitted brine-cured kalamata olives
2 large eggs
1 teaspoon freshly ground black pepper
1 cup (2 sticks) unsalted butter, melted
Sixteen 14 x 18-inch sheets phyllo pastry, covered with a sheet of parchment or wax paper and then a damp kitchen towel (see note on page 45)

▓ In the bowl of a food processor, combine the cheese, olives, eggs, and pepper and pulse to form a coarse paste, scraping down the bowl as necessary. Set aside.

▓ Brush two rimmed baking sheets with some of the butter. Set aside.

▓ Transfer one sheet of phyllo to a work surface (keep the remaining phyllo covered) and brush it with some butter. Top it with another sheet, brushing it with butter.

▓ Use a sharp knife to cut the sheets widthwise into 4 pieces, each 14 x 4½ inches. Spoon 1 tablespoon of the cheese and olive mixture in a line along one of the 4½-inch sides, leaving a ¾-inch border from the three edges. Roll the end of the phyllo up and over the filling, continuing to roll it into a tight, neat bundle for about one-third of the length of the phyllo. Fold in the side edges, then continue rolling the length of the phyllo. Arrange the rolled cigar, seam side down, on one of the prepared baking sheets and brush the cigar with butter. Repeat with the remaining phyllo and cheese and olive mixture, making about 32 rolls. Place the baking sheets in the freezer for at least an hour. (You can freeze the cigars, covered, for up to a week.)

▓ Preheat the oven to 350°F.

▓ Remove the cigars from the freezer and bake until golden brown, 30 to 35 minutes. Serve hot or at room temperature.

sharp cheddar and bresaola melt

This is simply, brilliantly, nothing more than a dressed-up grilled cheese sandwich, perhaps one of life's most perfect foods.

But while a plain grilled cheese sandwich would be okay with a glass of Cabernet, this one really works, thanks to the addition of savory bresaola, bright Dijon mustard, and either sun-dried tomatoes or arugula. (Although that last ingredient—sun-dried tomatoes or arugula—gives you two pretty different options, they both add color and Cabernet-friendly notes, the tomatoes being richly savory and the arugula having a slight nuttiness.) • SERVES 4

2 tablespoons unsalted butter, room temperature
6 slices sourdough bread
4½ teaspoons Dijon mustard
4 ounces extra-sharp Cheddar cheese, thinly sliced
¼ cup drained oil-packed julienned sun-dried tomatoes, or 2 cups loosely packed arugula (about 1 ounce)
24 thin slices bresaola (about 5 ounces) (see page 148) or Italian dry salami (3 to 4 ounces)

▨ Spread the butter on one side of each slice of bread, dividing it evenly. Place 3 slices, buttered side down, on a work surface and spread the unbuttered side with the mustard, dividing it evenly. Top with the cheese, sun-dried tomatoes or arugula, and bresaola, dividing them evenly. Top with the remaining bread, buttered side up.

▨ Heat a large nonstick skillet over medium-low heat. Add the sandwiches, cover, and cook, in batches if necessary, until golden brown and the cheese is melted, 3 to 5 minutes per side. (You can also cook the sandwiches on a panini grill for 3 to 5 minutes.)

▨ Cut the sandwiches into quarters and serve hot.

FOOD & WINE TIP Sharp Cheddar has a great affinity to Cabernet Sauvignon—as do blue cheeses, aged cheeses, Parmesan, and sometimes stinky cheeses.

steak, porcini, and parmesan risotto

Even if you've never cooked risotto, you've probably heard about how "hard" it is to make. I put that word in quotes because, actually, it's not difficult at all. Making risotto is as easy as heating some broth, sautéing some onions and maybe a few other vegetables, adding rice, and then stirring for 15 or 20 minutes, adding a little broth at a time. Yes, good risotto does require near-constant stirring. But—what's so hard about stirring?

More accurately, then, risotto requires neither a lot of skill nor a lot of time. Just tending. During which you stir.

The stirring is actually the thing that gives risotto its trademark richness. As you stir, the friction of those rice grains rubbing up against each other scratches off the starch, thickening your liquid. If you didn't stir, you'd have rice in broth. But because you do, you have luscious, creamy heaven in a bowl.

Counter that minor inconvenience with the fact that risotto is basically a one-pot meal. (Okay, two pots if you count the saucepan that keeps your broth hot.) So in exchange for your attentiveness, cleanup is quick and easy.

The point is, don't be daunted by risotto. Its reputation as a fussy food that only a brave or experienced home chef can master is utterly unfounded. And the final result is more than worth the "effort."

This recipe serves eight as a pasta first course. If you want to make it for a finger-foods party, serve it in big, fancy spoons—get a bunch inexpensively at a restaurant supply store—for one- or two-bite mouthfuls. • SERVES 8

6 cups reduced-sodium beef broth
¼ cup extra virgin olive oil
1 onion, cut into ¼-inch dice
1½ teaspoons coarse kosher salt, or more to taste
½ teaspoon freshly ground black pepper, or more to taste
1½ cups Arborio rice
¼ ounce dried porcini mushrooms, torn into ¼-inch pieces (you should have about 3 tablespoons)
½ cup Cabernet Sauvignon, or other dry red wine
1⅓ cups thinly sliced cooked steak (about 8 ounces) (see below)
¾ cup grated Parmesan cheese (4 to 5 ounces), plus more for serving
About 2 tablespoons balsamic vinegar, ideally good-quality aged balsamic

■ In a medium saucepan over high heat, bring the broth to a boil. Reduce the heat to very low, adjusting to keep the broth just below a simmer.

■ In a large saucepan or small stockpot over medium heat, warm the olive oil. Add the onion, salt, and pepper and cook, stirring occasionally, until the onion is very soft, 6 to 8 minutes (adjust the heat, if necessary, to avoid browning). Add the rice and mushrooms and stir until all the rice grains are coated with oil. Add the wine and cook, stirring, until the wine is absorbed. Ladle in enough hot broth to barely cover the rice, about 1½ cups. Stir constantly until almost all of the broth has been absorbed, adjusting the heat to maintain a simmer. Continue adding broth, about ½ cup at a time, and stirring almost constantly, adding more broth when almost all of the previous addition has been absorbed.

■ After 15 or 20 minutes, taste the rice for doneness. It should be tender but firm, with no chalkiness in the center, and the overall mixture should be slightly looser than you would ultimately like it (the final addition of cheese will thicken it). If it's not done, continue cooking, adding broth, and stirring until the rice is done (you may not need all of the broth).

■ Remove the risotto from the heat and stir in the steak and ¾ cup of the cheese. Taste, ideally with your wine, and add more salt and/or pepper if you like.

■ Serve the risotto hot, drizzled with the vinegar. Pass additional cheese at the table. (You can also pass a bottle of balsamic vinegar at the table.)

NOTE This recipe is good for using up leftover steak, but if you don't have any, simply grill, broil, or pan-sauté a seasoned 10- to 12-ounce steak for about 3½ minutes per side for medium rare. Let it rest about 5 minutes before slicing. You can use any type of steak you like, but a richly marbled one, like New York or rib-eye, will be best with the wine.

pan-seared rib-eye ribbons with cabernet mustard sauce

One of the easiest ways to dress up a pan-seared piece of meat, poultry, or fish is to use the browned bits left in the bottom of the skillet to make a sauce. And by "sauce" I don't mean a big, thick gravy. I'm talking about a few spoonfuls of something flavorful and wet that will enhance your simply prepared main attraction.

The steaks in this recipe get just that sort of easy-but-tasty treatment. After they're cooked and are set aside to rest, the skillet is deglazed with a little wine. The heat, the liquid, and a gentle scrape of your spoon or spatula release the caramelized bits on the bottom, which give their flavor to the sauce. A little butter thickens and sweetens, while a little mustard adds brightness. And just that easily, you've got a wonderful, flavorful, "gourmet" dish, way beyond a plain old steak.

This recipe serves four as a small plate or as a sharing-sized portion of a main course, but it will also serve two as an entrée. • SERVES 4

Two 8- to 10-ounce rib-eye steaks, about 1 inch thick
1 teaspoon coarse kosher salt
¾ teaspoon freshly ground black pepper
1 tablespoon extra virgin olive oil
½ cup Cabernet Sauvignon, or other dry red wine
2 tablespoons unsalted butter, cut into 3 or 4 pieces
1 tablespoon stone-ground mustard
2 teaspoons chopped fresh chives

▓ Sprinkle both sides of the steaks with the salt and pepper. Set aside.

▓ In a large skillet over medium-high heat, warm the olive oil. Add the steaks and cook to desired doneness, about 3½ minutes per side for medium rare. Transfer the steaks to a cutting board and let rest, loosely covered with foil, for 5 minutes.

▓ Meanwhile, return the skillet to medium heat. Stir in the wine, scraping up any browned bits in the bottom of the skillet, and cook until the wine is just a thin layer in the skillet, about 2 minutes. Remove the skillet from the heat and add the butter, stirring until the butter is melted. Stir in the mustard. Set the skillet aside.

▓ Cut the steak diagonally into ½-inch slices. Fan the slices out on a platter or individual plates. Drizzle with the mustard sauce, sprinkle with the chives, and serve hot.

index